THE

GIFT

GIVER

Love + Light!

THE
GIFT
GIVER

JENNIFER
HAWKINS

A TRUE STORY

EMERALD
BOOK CO.

Published by Emerald Book Company
Austin, Texas
www.emeraldbookcompany.com

Distributed by Emerald Book Company

For ordering information or special discounts for bulk purchases, please contact Emerald Book Company at PO Box 91869, Austin, TX 78709, 512.891.6100.

Design and composition by Greenleaf Book Group LLC and Alex Head
Cover design by Greenleaf Book Group LLC

Publisher's Cataloging-In-Publication Data
(Prepared by The Donohue Group, Inc.)
Hawkins, Jennifer (Jennifer Lynne), 1969-
  The gift giver : a true story / Jennifer Hawkins.—1st ed.
  p. ; cm.
  ISBN: 978-1-934572-80-1
  1. Hawkins, Jennifer (Jennifer Lynne), 1969—Family. 2. Bereavement—Psychological aspects. 3. Husbands—Death—Psychological aspects. 4. Loss (Psychology) 5. Widows—United States—Psychology. I. Title.
  BF575.G7 H29 2011
  155.9/37   2011923306

Part of the Tree Neutral® program, which offsets the number of trees consumed in the production and printing of this book by taking proactive steps, such as planting trees in direct proportion to the number of trees used: www.treeneutral.com

Printed in the United States of America on acid-free paper

TreeNeutral®

11 12 13 14   10 9 8 7 6 5 4 3 2 1

First Edition

For our boys

NOTE TO READER

I believe these events happened to me . . .
and are true.
But truth is a very personal thing.
And my truth may or may not be your truth.

My intention is to share with you the experiences,
lessons, and insights
that changed my and my boys' lives forever,
in the hope that they will deeply enrich your life.

I wrote this book for you.

—Jennifer

THE PERFECT DAY

I woke up at 6:40 after sleeping soundly for an unheard-of nine hours. I looked over to see if Mark was awake. He was, and he smiled at me.

Just then, Connor and Brannon came running into the bedroom and jumped on our bed. Mark rolled over and held me in his arms while the boys pulled open the covers and snuck in. They began to tease Mark to play with them and let go of me. He didn't.

I relaxed into his arms and enjoyed the sensation of my husband, my boys, and me, snuggled together: intimate, comfortable, a family. I wanted the moment to last forever.

Later in the day, Mark and I went out to lunch. While we were ordering our food I said, "I'm so excited for our trip to Cozumel next month."

Mark said, "I know! Can you believe we will be swimming in the ocean in five weeks?"

I laughed and said, "I hope it isn't like our honeymoon!"

Mark laughed too while we both remembered that escapade.

Then Mark said, "We need to get the boys' passports."

I'd forgotten about that. I said, "Did you find out what we need to do?"

He said, "Yes, we both have to take them to the counter at the passport place and bring all four of our birth certificates. Then they will put a rush on them and we'll get them in time for our trip."

I said, "Should we do that tomorrow after we pick them up from school?"

He said, "That's exactly what I was thinking."

After lunch, Mark went to work downstairs in his office while I went upstairs to my office to check on a few things. But I couldn't concentrate. I went down and knocked on Mark's door. I wanted to talk with him about the changes in our marriage and how happy I was since we had started counseling, but when I saw the look on his face, I simply walked over and sat on his lap.

He held me in his arms for a couple of minutes and then took my hand and, without a word, led me upstairs to our bedroom. After working in the house together for five years, that was a first.

When the boys got home from school, we took them on a bike ride around the neighborhood and then cooked dinner together. Before we started eating we did our "five seconds": We held hands and were quiet for five seconds, and then each of us said what we were thankful for.

The boys were thankful for their food, as usual. Mark said he was thankful for his family, as usual. I said I was thankful for Mark.

While I was doing the dishes, Mark took the boys upstairs and gave them their baths. Later I walked in to brush my teeth. Brannon looked up at me from the tub with a face full of bubbles and made a big "smack" with his lips as if he were kissing me. I just laughed.

Mark read to the boys and put them in bed. He told them stories about his grandparents, Big Granny and Big Poppy, and their dogs, Elmo and Mandy, who were up in heaven playing.

After he finished, Mark came downstairs, and we cuddled on the couch and watched a couple of episodes of *Friday Night Lights*. Typically we would go to bed around ten o'clock, but tonight, at ten thirty, Mark asked if I wanted to watch just one more show.

I said, "No, I'm pretty tired." He seemed kind of sad but let it go.

When I got up to our bathroom, I looked at the mirror and started laughing. Mark had taped a note there and written it as if it were from Brannon to me. It said, "Smack! I love you, Brannon." It even had a set of lips drawn on the note.

As we were lying in bed, a fulfilling sense of peace and warmth came over me. I realized that I felt similarly to the day we had gotten married. Everything felt right. I remembered that day and how the night before, a storm had come rolling through the hills. The excitement of our wedding had been as thick in the air as the smell of the rain. Now the joyful anticipation of our future life together rolled through me like a strong, sure current. Mark scooted over, held me for a while, gave me a kiss, and said, "I love you."

"I love you too, sweetie."

But then he added, "No, I *really, really* love you."

This was the first time he had ever said it quite that way, and it felt delicious.

I looked up at him and said, "I really, really love you too."

The last thing I remember thinking before I drifted off to sleep was, "I am so excited for the next year of our lives. I can't wait to spend it together with this amazing man and our family."

DAY TWO

When I woke up, I could see the light starting to come through the window but decided to close my eyes and enjoy the silence and peace that only comes before the first words of the day are spoken.

After a few moments, I heard Connor through the monitor, singing in his room. His soft young voice made me grin, and I thought, "How am I so lucky, to wake up this way?"

I slowly opened my eyes and turned to glance over my shoulder. I noticed that Mark was still sleeping, so I gently got up out of bed and looked at the clock: it was 6:28. I tiptoed over and turned off the monitors, then sneaked out of our room, quietly closing the door so Mark could get a few more precious minutes of shut-eye.

I walked down the hall, and when I opened the door to Connor's room I saw his hair—so blond it was almost white—poking out from under the covers. Then he pushed the comforter aside, looked up at me with his angelic, sky-blue eyes, smiled, and said, "Hi Mommy. Is today a school day?"

"Yes it is."

I watched as a huge smile spread across his bright face.

Then he said, "You know, I told my friend Isabella that when she chases me around the playground that if she catches me and grabs me hard, I will keep running. But if she grabs me softly, I'll stop."

My eyes widened at the thought of our five-year-old being softly hugged by a very sweet, beautiful girl in his class. I was curious to find out if the hug actually occurred, so I asked, "So, what did she do?"

Connor said with a sly but slightly shy look on his face, "She grabbed me softly."

My heart melted a little with his fragile and truly honest expression of love.

About that time I heard Brannon push open Connor's door. His fingers came in first, then tufts of his slept-on, crumpled, brownish-red hair, just like Mark's, appeared. Finally he peeked around the door with his chocolate-brown eyes.

He looked at Connor and me with a twinkle in his eye. Then he casually walked over to the window, put his fingers in the shutters, pushed them open, and exclaimed, "It's already morning!" with the enthusiasm only a three-year-old can muster before seven a.m.

I mirrored his delighted attitude. "Yes it is!"

He turned around, strolled over, and hopped up on the bed with Connor and me. The three of us cuddled and giggled while I read them a couple of their favorite stories.

Pretty soon I realized it was almost seven and we needed to start getting ready for school. I said, "Let's go see if Daddy is up!"

Both boys looked at me excitedly, flashed grins, and then took off in a sprint down the hall toward our bedroom.

When they got to our room it took them a few moments to open the door, and during that time I almost caught up to them. I was about three steps from the room when I heard both boys jump up on the bed and Brannon say, "Daddy, Daddy!" Then there was silence.

For a split second I thought it was strange for Mark to be so quiet. Usually he would get very excited when the boys ran into the room and jumped up on the bed. Then as I walked into the room I heard Connor worriedly say, "Mommy, Daddy isn't moving."

IRONY

My heart started pounding against my ribs as I broke into a run.

When I got to the side of the bed, I realized Mark was not okay. "Dear God, what if he's cold?" I thought.

I wasn't breathing when I reached over gently to touch his arm. When I did, it felt like it pushed back. I thought, "Is he kidding around?"

I looked closer and realized one of his eyes was open a tiny bit but not moving at all. Then the thoughts flooded in: "Oh my God! He's not kidding! This is not a joke. He's gone! No!"

I could not believe it! I started to hyperventilate. My only thought at that instant was, "Somehow I have to protect the boys."

"Hey guys," I said, gathering my courage so I could speak in a normal tone of voice, "let's go back in Connor's room for a little while and play so I can see what's going on with Daddy."

I took each of their little hands, helped them off the bed, and led them into the hall. As we approached Connor's room, Brannon looked up at me and asked, "Is Daddy dead?"

I didn't say anything; I didn't trust myself to utter a word. And what could I say when I was pretty sure he was, and I couldn't take in a breath?

In a complete panic inside but trying to hold myself together on the outside for the boys, I shut them in Connor's room and said, "Play for a little bit; I'll be right back."

I ran into our bedroom as fast as I could. I felt Mark's arm and touched his forehead gently. There was nothing I could do. He was not only much colder than he should have been, but he was already stiff. I grabbed my stomach—so hard that I left a bruise. In my head was a furious and denying, "Are you kidding me!?! After yesterday!?!" aching to be screamed to the universe as loud as my voice would go. But I couldn't let it out for fear of scaring the boys.

I didn't know what to do. The only thing I could think of was to call 911. I ran into my office and picked up the phone and dialed.

One ring . . . two rings . . . an eternity. I felt sick to my stomach. This could not be happening! When the woman finally picked up, she asked if it was a fire, an ambulance, or a police need. I didn't know what to say—I couldn't bring myself to say the blunt phrase in my mind: "He's dead." What came out instead was, "I think my husband is not alive anymore."

As I said the words, silent tears started to gush out of my eyes. She asked me where he was. I said, "He's on our bed." She asked how I found him; I told her. She asked if we had a defibrillator. I said, "No."

Then she said, "You need to perform CPR on him. Take him off the bed and put him on the floor."

I couldn't do it. I said a little louder, "He isn't here anymore."

She kept saying I had to try to do CPR on him, and I kept telling her I couldn't. Why didn't she understand he was dead? My God . . . my husband was dead.

I was breathing so fast I couldn't feel my body, other than the horrible tightness in my stomach that was forming while I tried to stave off the loud sobs that were coming, a sound I didn't want the boys to hear. The tears, however, couldn't be stopped and were flowing silently and hard now.

She asked me if there was someone close by who could come to our house quickly. I told her that our neighbor Deb could probably come over. I couldn't remember her number, and my hands were shaking so bad I had trouble turning the page of my address book. I finally found it and told her the number.

She started back in on me to try CPR. I couldn't get her to understand that there was no point in CPR. I'd had a CPR class in college, and I knew that it would do no good.

The woman on the phone told me to go downstairs and unlock the front door. I didn't understand why. She said, "So your neighbor and the emergency people can get in if you can't be at the door."

Oh, right. But how could I go downstairs? The boys might come out of their room. I ran down as fast as I could, unlocked the door, then ran right back up and stood in the hall, glancing back and forth between our room and the door to Connor's room, praying it wouldn't open.

Then she asked me if we had a dog. I *really* didn't understand why she was asking that question. I gave her an exasperated "Yes."

She said to put it somewhere so when the ambulance got there it wouldn't bark at the paramedics. Oh.

I ran upstairs. Then I thought, "Where is Dallas?" She slept by our bed at night, but I couldn't imagine she would be there now. I walked slowly into our room. For a split second I looked at Mark, then down at the floor. Why was Dallas lying by the side of the bed as if nothing had happened? I called to her and she jumped up. I took hold of her collar, ran downstairs, and put her outside.

Then I heard the sirens in the distance and I froze. I instantly hated that sound. It used to bring me excitement, a chance to show the boys the flashing lights. But now, the sirens brought something totally different.

DEB

I heard a knock at the door. It was Deb. Thank God; I was so tired of arguing with the lady on the phone, I handed it to Deb. I told her the boys were in Connor's room and asked her to go be with Mark so the boys wouldn't be able to see him.

Deb walked into our bedroom while she was on the phone. She looked at Mark and was shocked. The operator had only told her that there was a medical emergency, not that Mark had died.

Desperate to get the boys out of the house, I ran out the front door and over to the house of our neighbor, Nathalie. I banged on the door, and when she finally opened it, I told her I thought Mark had died. Her mouth hung open, and she moved toward me a little. I instantly took her arm and began pulling her to our home. I said, "Please, please, please, just watch the boys for me." She followed me into the house and got the boys downstairs just as the paramedics walked in.

By the time I got back upstairs, one of the paramedics was walking out of our bedroom. He looked a little familiar, but I shook it off. He looked toward the floor and said, "Yes ma'am, you were right; there is nothing we can do."

Then he just stood there.

Now that someone was with the boys, I wanted to go in and see Mark, but the paramedic blocked my way and said, "I'm sorry, but you can't go in there." Anger welled up in me. I had not spent even a minute with Mark. Why couldn't I go in?

Then I understood. This was an unexplained death of a man who was not old enough to die in his sleep . . . a potential crime scene. They had to consider that *I'd* done this to him.

Deb was talking with the paramedic. I looked up at him briefly and his eyes caught mine. There was grief there and something else . . . guilt, perhaps. I didn't know what to make of it. Maybe he felt bad for having to keep me out of the room.

I sat down on the floor and grabbed my legs as hard as I could. My mind was racing, and my breathing rate was off the charts. I could not believe this was all happening. I was scared, sad, angry, and in shock all at once.

I HATE YOU

I heard Nathalie downstairs getting the boys dressed and packing up food for them to take to her house. I was thankful when I heard their voices but . . . they were so innocent. This would destroy their world. I heard them walk out of the house with Nathalie. I didn't have to hide anymore, but I couldn't move. I was crying so hard and breathing so fast I was scared to stand up.

My whole world was smashing down in front of my eyes and I couldn't think, feel, or breathe right. I just sat there on the floor outside our bedroom with my arms wrapped as tightly as I could around my legs, sobbing and gasping for air. I kept looking toward our bed and trying to be with Mark, at least from afar.

Within a few minutes the house was swarmed with police, the Medical Examiner, Victim Services, detectives, and even more paramedics, it seemed. I don't know how long I sat there. I remember Deb standing next to me and asking questions of the people who came near us; I remember her rubbing my neck and back. I was still in my robe and, despite being in shock, was starting to feel uncomfortable with all of the strangers in my home.

Someone told Deb to take me to her house. Since the detectives wouldn't let me go back in our bedroom, Deb had to go in my closet to get some clothes for me. I knew this was probably because of some protocol, but to not allow me into my own closet felt cruel. I didn't want to leave the house; I felt as if I were abandoning Mark. But Deb told me they were not going to let me stay. She helped me up and sat with me while I got dressed in our guest room. When I walked outside with Deb holding my arm as if I were eighty years old, I looked up, and the sun blinded me for a moment. I was staring at a perfectly blue sky. It was as if God were laughing, and I hated God at that moment. My love, my husband, my children's father had been taken from me. I wanted to scream, "*I hate you!*" at the top of my lungs. But there were people everywhere.

When I was walking over to Deb's house, everything looked fake. The houses seemed like props in a movie; the trees looked plastic. The world was not as it had been before. I was scared people would see me—I wanted to hide.

DECISIONS

When we walked in the door at Deb's house, she said, "Jen, who should I call?"

I quickly said, "Nobody."

In my head I was thinking I couldn't tell anyone. If I told someone in my family, then this would all be true; Mark would really be gone.

She said, "You need to call your mom."

But I couldn't do it; I told her it was too early in California.

"Your mom will want to be on the next flight out here."

I realized she was probably right. "Okay, but I can't talk to anyone."

She called my mom, who got on the next flight.

She also called my dad, who lived about two miles away. Within minutes the front door opened and he came rushing over to me.

The moment I saw his face I crumbled inside, as images of Mark laughing and joking with my dad over the last eight years came flooding into my mind.

He took me in his arms and held me as if he would never let go; he didn't say a word. This was unreal—it could not be true. But I realized that because my dad was there, it was—it simply was true. There was nothing I could do to change the fact that Mark was gone. No notice, no warning, no chance to say goodbye . . . just gone. One moment he was there, the next he was not.

My dad held me for the longest time while I cried. I think he would have stood there forever if I had needed him to. Deb came in the room and asked if she could make me something to eat. I thought, "Food? Can I even think about it? It seems so unnecessary, so trivial, such a fake pleasure within all of this pain." I shook my head no.

She went into the kitchen and made me some eggs anyway. Deb, like everyone who would be in my space over the next weeks, felt that she had to take care of me. But Deb was the first.

She brought over the eggs and I looked at the plate. It was disgusting. I had no appetite; there was no way I could lift food up to my mouth. I felt as if I were made of stone; I could hardly move, much less eat.

While I was staring at the eggs, the doorbell rang. Two women who said they were with Victim Services came inside and asked me when I was going to go see the boys. Connor and Brannon were still over at Nathalie's house playing, and it had been an hour or so since I'd seen them. The women also wanted to know if I was going to send the boys to school. I didn't know what to do.

At that point another neighbor, Lydia, walked in the living room. She had three children, two who were the same age as my boys, but I didn't understand why she was there. I hadn't known it before, but she was a social worker; she had all of the answers I needed. She sat down on the couch and said, "Don't send the boys to school, and wait a little while before you go see them. They don't need to see you like this."

What a relief—someone else could make decisions. I certainly couldn't.

The Victim Services people started telling me what was happening. They said that the Medical Examiner was at the house with Mark and was trying to determine the cause of death.

Right—something *caused* this. One of them said that they would most likely not be able to determine it that morning.

They said there would need to be an autopsy because of Mark's young age. My mind went automatically to the thought: "An autopsy? What does that mean? I've never known anyone who had an autopsy. Are they going to have to cut him up? My *sweetie*? God, how am I going to handle this?"

I learned that when the detectives were finished searching our house that the Medical Examiner would take Mark to the place where they would do the autopsy. They told me that they found his driver's license and that it indicated he was an organ donor. However, they told me that the autopsy would prevent him from being able to donate any organs.

Oh God, they *would* be cutting him up!

But then I heard one of them say, "But his eyes . . ." I looked at her with distrust.

She asked if it would be okay with me if they took the corneas from his eyes and donated them to someone who could not see. She said the autopsy would not damage them.

What did she say? They want his eyes? His eyes . . . Really?

Tears were streaming out of *my* eyes. How many hours had I spent looking into Mark's eyes? Could I let someone else have them? What would that do to his face? Was this real? Was I actually making decisions about my husband's body?

Already knowing what Mark would say, I looked at my dad. I knew that Mark always said yes to anything that might be of help to another person. I, however, didn't know what to say.

The Victim Services women told me that they had to know very soon or else the corneas would not be able to be saved. They said it was very lucky that the death was not very long ago, but if they were going to be able to retain the corneas' use for another person, they would have to move fast.

I couldn't speak. I looked at my dad again. He nodded his head.

Somehow I said the word, "Okay."

Mark's eyes . . . his beautiful, soft, loving eyes . . . I could not appreciate the gift right then. The women pushed a form in front of me and I signed it, feeling like a traitor.

Then it hit me: They had said they were taking him away! I told them I wanted to see him before they took him. One of them said, "You can't do that, ma'am. It is against the rules of the investigation."

I started to panic. Not only had my husband just died suddenly and unexpectedly in his sleep, but I wouldn't even get to see him and tell him goodbye before they took him away? I fell apart.

My dad looked up at her and said simply, "If that is your final say, we need to speak with a supervisor."

One of the women stood up and made a call to her boss. About thirty minutes later her phone rang. When she got off the phone, she said they were going to make an exception and that it was extremely rare, but for some reason they were going to let me see him. She said I would not be able to touch him, though.

I sat in Deb's living room, wondering what I should be doing. What would a normal person who could still feel and think do right now? I wondered. I looked at the plate of eggs . . . No. I looked at Deb, and she tried to smile at me. I was scared I would start to hyperventilate again, so I didn't even respond. I felt the side of my dad's body next to mine as he sat beside me on the couch; he was warm—not like Mark. He moved—not like Mark. And he loved me . . . but not the same way that Mark did.

The Victim Services lady had walked out of the room. When she returned she said, "We can go over to the house now."

I was a little surprised, thinking it would take longer. I felt a twinge in my stomach; was I ready for this? I looked over at my dad. I'm sure there was fear in my eyes. He stood up and took my hand to help me up.

We walked out the door. There were only two houses between Deb's and mine. It was still a bright and gleaming morning. As we made our way up the street we walked by my dad's truck. Something seemed out of place. Then I realized what it was: The truck was parallel parked, but its front tire was up on the curb in my neighbor's lawn.

We got to our house and were walking up the driveway. An ambulance was backed into our driveway, its back doors open. "God, it's for Mark," I thought. I slowed down a little, and my dad noticed. He stopped and said, "Is this okay?"

I just stood there. I looked up at the sky and tried to stop the tears from overflowing; I took a deep breath.

"I'm okay," I said, looking at my dad. "Let's go."

As we were walking up the steps to our house, I realized it wasn't our house anymore. I realized Mark would never open the door for me again; he would never hold my hand again. *Nothing* would ever be the same as it was a few hours ago.

GONE

My dad opened the door, went in, and waited for me. With absolute determination, I forced my body through that door and into my home. As I walked in, I saw the paramedics bringing Mark down the stairs on a stretcher.

As they were coming down the stairs, they jarred him really hard, and my first instinct was to say, "*Be careful!*" Then I realized that there wasn't any reason for them to be careful; my heart grabbed even harder in my chest.

They stopped at the bottom of the stairs, and I forced myself to walk over. The paramedic who had blocked my bedroom said, "You can see him, but you aren't allowed to touch him."

I nodded my head, though I didn't understand why I couldn't touch him. What did they think I was going to do?

It took all of my effort to turn my head to look down at Mark. The first thing I noticed was that he was still wearing one of the nose strips he used to keep from snoring. I was instantly furious. Couldn't they let him have some dignity? Why hadn't they taken that off? I would have. Anger welled up in me, then stopped almost as soon as it came on. Here he was—my deceased husband. I didn't know what to do or expect. I stood there looking at his face; he looked like he was sleeping.

I stood next to Mark and closed my eyes, thinking of all the love he had brought into the world and how I would miss him so dearly. I let the tears fall from my eyes, down my face, and off my chin to the floor. It was uncomfortable not putting my hands on him, not feeling the warmth of him, not being held gently by his loving hands as I would have been if he'd been there. As I stood there and silently told him how I felt, I realized that my beautiful man was not there. His body was there; his spirit was not. I had not expected being in his presence to cause the emptiness to hit me so hard. That moment—when I realized he was truly gone—will be etched in my memory forever. The pain spread through my body in a wave. I clutched my stomach as hard as I could with one hand and covered my forehead and eyes with the other. I could hardly stand.

I looked over toward my dad, who moved toward me, and I heard someone say, "We need to go."

I nodded. Then I watched as they wheeled him out of our home and out of my life forever. I even watched as they took him to the ambulance.

Mark had always told me that when you love somebody, you watch them go; you don't go back in the house after you have waved at them in the driveway. And so, I watched them drive him away.

As I was still looking out the door at the empty street, a detective came up behind me and said, "I have some questions I need to ask you."

I turned around and glared at him. In that instant, I hated him. I said, "*Can you just give me one minute!* They just took my dead husband away!"

He looked a little shocked and scared. Then his eyes softened and he said, "Yes ma'am. I'm so sorry." I sat down on the porch steps and started to cry. I realized I didn't hate the detective; I hated this whole morning.

After a few minutes I walked in the house and went into the living room. I had to sit down, so I slumped into the couch Mark and I had picked out together several years before. There were so many people around, but I felt completely alone. It seemed as if everyone was watching me, yet when I looked in their eyes, they looked away as if they couldn't face what I was experiencing. I didn't care.

The detective slowly came over to stand in front of me and asked everything from "What did you have for dinner?" to "Did your husband take any of the herbal supplements we found?" He even asked, "When did you last have intercourse?"

As I answered his questions like a robot, I felt invaded, sad, exhausted, angry, and numb—all at the same time.

When he ran out of questions, I had a few for him. He said I was free to do whatever I wanted, and I thought, "Well, why *wouldn't* I be?"

But I said, "Can I go upstairs?"

He looked at me as if he didn't know what I was asking.

"Is it a mess?" I asked.

"No, everything is as you left it."

THE BOYS

After the detective and Victim Services left, I paced around the house for another hour or so. I didn't know how to go tell Connor and Brannon what had happened. How could I actually form the words on my lips to tell them they didn't have a father anymore?

My neighbor Lydia had already gone over and checked on them twice. When she came back the third time she said, "Jen, you need to go over there. They are expecting you. You *will* have the strength to do this."

I hoped and prayed she was right.

Gathering all my willpower, I walked over and knocked on my neighbor's front door. She answered. I heard the boys playing in the back of the house. The sound of their sweet and innocent voices was a blessing. After Nathalie hugged me, I walked back to the playroom and stood at the door watching them for a minute before they saw me. I savored the normalcy of the moment. The fact that they could *play* right then gave me some strength to speak the words I had to.

Then I remembered something!

Four or five nights ago I had been putting Connor in bed and he said to me, "Mommy, I want to be one of the lucky ones."

I didn't know what he was talking about, so I said, "What do you mean?"

"When Daddy was driving us to school today, he told me and Brannon that only lucky people die in their sleep."

As I thought about that conversation we'd had just days before, I silently said, "Thank you." I took a few big, slow breaths and walked in.

I now knew I could do what had to be done. I sat down on the floor right next to them and softly said, "Hi guys."

When they both looked at me, I took another deep breath. "How are you doing? Have you had fun over here?"

They both said, "Yes."

"I need to talk to you about something, okay?"

They nodded their heads.

"Do you remember how Daddy said that only lucky people die in their sleep?"

They answered again in unison, "Yes."

I was amazed they both answered so quickly. I was scared to stop for fear that I couldn't get the words out at all, so I immediately said, "Well, Daddy is one of the lucky ones."

With a slightly confused expression on his face, Connor said, "Daddy died?"

I looked at him and gently but very clearly said, "Yes."

Then I turned toward Brannon.

He looked like he was about to crumble. His lower lip started to shake, and he softly asked, "Who will carry me around?"

I immediately answered, "Me, forever."

He stepped toward me slowly and I pulled him into my arms.

After I held them both for several minutes, the three of us went back over to our house together.

I wondered if I should take the boys up into the room where Mark died. I decided I didn't want our bedroom to be a taboo area.

I started up the stairs, and the boys instinctively followed me. We went into our bedroom, and I opened the curtains to let in the light and positive energy. I wasn't angry at the bright day anymore; I had a use for it now.

I made a point to sit on the bed. The boys crawled around me and even played a little with the sheets. They asked me question after question about Mark.

They wanted to know where he went. I said his body was at the hospital so that the doctors could find out why he died. And I told them that his soul, the part that was *really* Daddy, was up in heaven with Grandma Jean, his Granny and Poppy, and their dogs Elmo and Mandy, and that he would watch over us forever.

They asked if their Daddy could hear them.

I told them yes, that not only could he hear them, but that they could talk to him anytime they wanted. They asked how he could do that, and I said that his soul was like air now and could go anywhere. I said, "He can hear you even when you are by yourself."

The boys seemed okay when it was just the three of us—as though this was something that had happened to us together, and together we would heal. We stayed in the room for a long time.

Then as if life were calling, Brannon smiled at me, got up, and went to his bathroom to go potty. Connor followed him.

I started to walk out, but before I left the room, I looked at the bed where Mark had slept for the last eight years and never would again. I closed my eyes for a moment, then turned and followed the boys.

SNOWBALL

When I got downstairs, my dad and Deb were sitting at the table in the kitchen, talking. I felt like I needed some fresh air, so I went to the front door. Right when I opened the door to walk out, I saw Connor and Brannon's nanny Cheryl drive her Jeep up to the curb. I hadn't called her; how did she know?

I stood there on the front porch as she slammed on the brake, threw open her door, and ran up to me through the yard. Her whole face was smeared in tears, and she obviously had not even had a shower yet.

She clung to me and we dropped to our knees. I heard her say in my ear, "Oh God, Jen!"

I couldn't talk. I couldn't do anything but kneel there and cry with her. She was probably the one person who understood our family more than anyone in the whole world. She knew what an involved and wonderful dad Mark had been; she knew everything we had been through over the last three years. She was family.

When she finally released her grip a little and looked at me, she said, "I just can't believe it. Is it true?"

"Yes."

"Where are the boys? How are they? What can I do? I'm here for whatever you need, whenever you need it."

I knew she meant it.

As we walked in and went by the stairs, I grabbed her arm and said, "Will you please wash the sheets on our bed?"

All I thought of when I saw our bed was finding him and how he was gone. I had to get rid of that image somehow, and maybe this would help. But I couldn't actually go take the sheets off the bed myself; it seemed like a violation.

She looked at me, nodded, and went upstairs. After she came down and started the laundry, she walked into the living room and went to the boys.

When she kneeled down next to where they were playing, I saw a similar shift in her that had happened with me when I went in to tell them Mark had died: I saw her bright spirit and strength take over. She was calm, soothing, warm, and even smiling with the boys. They were in good hands, so I went to talk with my dad and Deb.

I sat down at the kitchen table and looked at them. "What have I missed?"

Deb said, "Your dad and I have been calling people to tell them what has happened."

I asked them who knew. She told me that they had contacted Mark's side of the family through his sister. I asked which one.

"Karen."

My heart sank. I knew that Karen would be a mess. I nodded my head, knowing there was nothing I could do to stop the ball of pain from plowing over everyone in its path, like a snowball gaining strength and speed as it rolls downhill.

Dad said, "I've called most of our side of the family, and people are spreading the word."

Okay. So, my biggest concern at this point was Mark's friends. I asked Dad and Deb if any of them had been contacted.

Dad said, "Yes, we called Julie, and she is calling the people she knows." Julie was Mark's co-worker; she would have some of the numbers of people who needed to know, but not all of them. I wondered if she had the phone numbers of Mark's hunting friends, some of whom Mark had known for thirty years, since they went to college together. They needed to know, immediately.

I stood up to go get the phone in order to call Julie, to see if she had called Sam. His family owned the ranch where Mark went hunting. As I was walking toward the phone, it rang.

I didn't know what to do. It was my business line, but I wasn't prepared to talk to anyone that didn't know. I walked over, picked up the phone, and looked at the caller ID.

It was Mark's dad. I stood there in shock. I couldn't talk to him.

I handed the phone to my dad and left the room. I couldn't stand it. The pain that hit me in the heart at that moment was too strong, and I knew words wouldn't come. It was too much to ask of myself. I felt ashamed and guilty that I wasn't strong enough, but I just couldn't do it. Mark's dad . . . No . . . No . . . No!

I saw Ray in my mind: his gentle smile, his sweet laugh, and his big, bear-hugging arms. I went upstairs to my room, thinking that my dad wouldn't come up there. I lay on the bed and wept.

MEMORIES

About five minutes later someone knocked on my bedroom door. I didn't say anything. Then I heard my dad say, "Ray wants to talk to you. He *needs* to talk to you."

I stood up and walked to the door with my hand clutching my stomach. I took the phone from my dad, sat down on the bed, and started crying.

I heard Ray's voice: "Sweetie ... Sweetie ... No ... We are coming right as soon as we can. Okay?"

I nodded my head.

He said, "Be gentle with yourself. Go be with the boys. We will see you in a few hours. We love you so much."

I sat there in silence with tears streaming down my face. I couldn't speak.

Finally I just said, "Ray."

He said, "I know."

And he did. He had just lost his beautiful wife Jean two and a half years ago. Now his *son*, too—his son! It was so unfair. How could he be so calm? I knew that under the calm he had to be destroyed.

I was so torn. I wanted him here; I needed his big bear hug. But I didn't know if I could stand to see Mark's eyes reflected in his father's. I didn't have a choice, though. The phone line went dead.

I dropped the receiver to the floor and curled up in a ball on my bed as the memories of my mother-in-law's death flooded over me.

In April of 2006 we got a call from Mark's dad, saying that Mark's stepmom Jean had lung cancer and wasn't going to live much longer. We immediately packed up the car and the boys and went to visit her.

When we walked into her hospital room, I was instantly struck by how calm she was. The nurses were suggesting hospice care already, and Ray was beside himself with worry and grief. Amid all of the chaos and fear, however, Jean seemed like an angel sitting in that bed.

She smiled constantly even though it was obvious she was exhausted and we knew she had to be in incredible pain. She even glowed; her skin looked almost luminescent and her color was better than I'd seen in years. I couldn't understand why she looked and acted so happy.

I was holding Brannon, and he kept reaching his little arms out to her like he wanted to hug her. I didn't want him to hurt her; there were wires and tubes going down the side of her arms and into her nose. He couldn't really walk yet, so I knew if I set him down he would crawl all over her and possibly cause a problem with the medical equipment. I asked her if it was okay to put him down on her bed.

She said, "Oh, yes! Please put him on my bed here with me."

I watched as he explored her. She seemed to be basking in his energy.

As we were getting ready to leave, a deep feeling of

sadness and gloom welled up in my chest. I knew I was going to have to say goodbye and knew deep down I'd never see her alive again. The thought gripped my heart, my gut. I leaned into her, put my arms around her gently, and held her. Then, with tears streaming down my face, hidden by my hair, I whispered in her ear, "It's been too short of a time."

She said, "Yes, but it's been wonderful. Be happy."

I had never lost anyone close to me before; those words took me by surprise. As she was preparing to go, it seemed as if her only thoughts were for those around her. It also felt as if she was enjoying her last hours and days, even though she knew they were numbered.

One night, a few weeks after Jean died, Mark and I were lying in bed reading, but my mind was wandering to thoughts of Jean. When I thought of her, it seemed as if she was right there with me. I even felt a slight tingle on my skin. It was not anything scary or strange—just the warm feeling of another person in the room, even though I knew that wasn't possible.

I told Mark that when we talked about her I could feel her warmth, and at times it seemed as if I could even hear her voice. I told him she seemed to be laughing and quite happy. Mark looked at me as if I were off my rocker, but I could tell in his heart he wanted to believe it was true; he wanted to believe she was okay.

The sound of the doorbell brought me back to the present . . . Deb came upstairs this time. She said, "Julie is here."

I stood up, wiped my face, and walked downstairs.

As I came down the last couple of steps, I saw her in the hall. She turned her head, looked at me, and said, "Oh, Jennifer."

I stepped off the last stair and almost collapsed in her arms. As far as co-workers go, Julie and I were close. She had worked with Mark before I met him, almost ten years ago. She had given him advice when he was dating me, and she and her family even came to our wedding. She was a dear friend.

"I just can't believe it," I said into her ear, my voice barely a whisper. "I don't know what to do. Will you help me?"

"Of course. Let's go in here and talk."

She was pointing to Mark's office. I hesitated for a moment. I had not been in his office yet, and I was not sure it was a good idea. She noticed my hesitation and said, "Or over here?" and pointed at a chair near the dining room table.

"No, let's go in the office." I'd never called it "the office;" it had always been "Mark's office." The words didn't feel right in my mouth. But I wanted to have some privacy, so we went in and closed the doors behind us.

I looked over at his desk and chair. There were pictures of Mark and his friends on the wall. I saw his diploma, pictures of him and the boys, pictures of me, photos from our wedding. It was almost too much to process.

I sat down in his chair, it was comforting. It was big and soft, and I felt as if maybe a little bit of Mark was there with us.

I looked up at Julie. "Who have you told?"

She said she'd called Mark's best friends, Randy and Sam, and that they would be here soon. I knew seeing them would be almost as difficult as seeing Mark's father, but, once again, I had no choice.

~

At about three that afternoon, there was a knock at the door. My dad went to answer it. I could see down the hallway to the front door from where I was sitting, and I watched as Randy walked in the house. I didn't think I had any tears left, but they came anyway. I looked down at the ground. Randy . . . He was Mark's best man in our wedding; Mark had been Randy's best man twice. The two of them had been friends for almost thirty years, and they had worked together in the same room for over seven years. They were like brothers.

Seeing Randy instantly triggered my memory of the story he told about Mark at our wedding.

One day, Mark and I left the office at the same time. Mark had gotten in his car and was about to drive off when I remembered something.

I waved him down and said, "Hey, buddy. Where did you get that tie? I've been eyeing it all day and I know it will go perfectly with a shirt I bought last week."

He said, "Neiman Marcus." Then he instantly started to take the tie off.

I said, "What are you doing?"

He handed me the tie through his window and said, "Here, you can have it."

I looked at him like he was crazy and said, "No, man! I don't want your tie. I just want to go buy one like it."

He said, "No really, take it. It's no big deal. I have at least twenty-five ties, and it will probably go better with your shirt than it does mine."

I argued with him, saying that I had money, I didn't need his tie, I could just drop by and buy one after work, and so on. Finally I couldn't think of any more reasons to refuse, and he was still holding the tie out for me to take.

As I drove off with a new tie lying on the front seat

of my car, I shook my head and thought, "Mark, you will never cease to amaze me."

The pain of Randy's loss throbbed through my bones. I stood up to hug him and felt him relax. I'm sure his three-hour drive had felt like walking on pins and needles.

He said, "Jen, I'm so sorry. What can I do to help?"

"Being here helps. But to tell you the truth, I'm really worried about the business," I told him. "I know Julie can probably hold down the fort, but can you help her, please?"

"Of course, I'll go talk with her and see what I can do."

I was relieved to have Randy in town. I knew he cared about the boys and me and could at least lead Julie in the right direction on some of the things that Mark took care of.

MOM

An hour or so later the front door opened again, and as if in slow motion, I watched my mom walk into the house. Meanwhile, my body stood up and dragged itself over to her and my throat croaked out, "Mom."

She was there. The mental and emotional props that had been supporting me gave way. With her there, I felt as if I could afford to completely break down—and I did. She took me in her arms and held me; she rocked me and stroked my hair until I could speak again. I don't know how long it took.

Finally I loosened the grip I had on her and whispered, "I just can't believe it."

She said, "I know."

"I can't even look around. There are pictures of us *everywhere*."

She nodded.

I could tell she was doing for me what I'd done for Connor and Brannon—being strong, being with me. She was letting me be whatever I needed to be in that moment.

I said, "Every time I look at the boys all I think is, 'you don't have a father anymore, how will you make it?'"

She nodded.

"Every time the phone rings, I think it's Mark."

"I know."

"I can't feel anything except hurt. My forehead hurts from crying. Why did this happen?"

She shook her head.

The phone rang. After a minute I heard my dad say, "Okay, I'll tell her."

He walked over to me and said, "Ray can't come until tomorrow. He's waiting for Mark's sister to drive to his house, and then they will be here late morning."

I was so relieved. I didn't think I could take one more person's arrival and the resulting flood of emotions and memories. Mark's dad would be the hardest to bear; I was thankful for a chance at some sleep before I had to face him.

THE FIRST NIGHT

I couldn't believe how tired I became as soon as my mom had walked in the door. It was as if my entire body had been tense the whole day; I felt as if I'd run a marathon. As soon as she let go of me I had to sit down.

The boys came over to me on the couch and asked if I'd read them a story. They were holding up *Duck on a Bike*, their favorite.

I said, "Sure, come on up and I'll read it."

Connor said, "We can cuddle, Mommy."

Yes. We could.

When I finished reading, I closed the book and held the boys in my arms for a little while. Brannon looked up at me and said, "I'm hungry."

Something somewhere in me smiled. There was such a familiarity to those words. Not much else that day had felt familiar. From Brannon's need came a glimmer of reality, life, and the future. It was grounding and comforting. I said, "Let's go see what Grandma cooked up."

After dinner Mark and I would usually trade off nights on who would bathe the boys and put them in bed. Mark had been so incredibly helpful. I felt as if I was about to take the nervous first step of a long hard journey I knew nothing about.

After their bath, the boys cuddled up to me and listened while I read their bedtime story.

When I finished, I began to feel a little panic in my chest. I realized I was scared to let them out of my sight—scared they would be scared to go to sleep; scared they would not sleep in their rooms; scared I wouldn't sleep. I tried to breathe and think.

I decided to act as if nothing were different and see what would happen. I told Connor to go into his room while I put Brannon in bed. After I kissed Brannon good night I said, "Night-night, I love you," as I always did.

"See you in the morning!"

"See you in the morning," I replied and closed the door slowly.

I stood there in the hall for a few seconds, wondering if I should leave. It seemed he had said, "See you in the morning" because he wanted to verify that he was safe and that we would really all be there in the morning. What a brilliant three-year-old. I turned and went into Connor's room.

When I kissed him goodnight he said, "Mommy, why did Daddy die?"

I had been waiting for and dreading this question. I hadn't thought how to answer it, so I decided to go with the truth. I said, "Sweetie, I don't know. The doctors are trying to figure that out. When I know, I will tell you."

"Okay."

I stayed with him in his room for a little while but knew if I stayed too long I would have trouble leaving. I stood up to go and he reached for me. He said, "Mommy, I'm scared."

I didn't know what to say. I was, too. I just stood there. I was the mom; I was supposed to be strong and supportive and know what to say. But where were the words?

I kneeled back down by his bed, hugged him, and said, "Me

too, sweetie, but everything is going to be okay. I'm here, Grandma is here, Brannon is here, and Dallas puppy is here."

"Okay."

I slowly left his room, went downstairs, and flopped down on the couch, exhausted. My mom was finishing up the dishes. She hung the dish towel on the oven door then came and sat on the couch with me. I moved over and put my head in her lap. She rubbed my forehead and hair for a while, and then she said, "Where do you want me to sleep?"

"With me."

"In the guest room?"

I thought about it for a minute, trying to decide how it would feel to be downstairs, away from the boys and in a bed that wasn't mine.

"No. I need to sleep in my bed."

THURSDAY

I tried to sleep that night, but once it was quiet, I kept thinking over and over, "*Why?*"

I was a light sleeper, and my mom's movements broke into the few precious moments when I'd finally drift off. By four o'clock in the morning I knew I wasn't going to sleep any more. I got up and went into my office.

I turned on my computer, and while it was booting up I looked out the window at the blackness. I was alone for the first time since Mark died. The darkness outside the window was ominous. However, being alone was a bit of a relief; I didn't have to worry about what anyone else was thinking or doing. I could just be, without others' judgment or grief filling up my space.

I thought, "Do I really want to get on the computer? I know there are going to be a bunch of emails that are condolences. Can I handle reading them right now?" I decided the answer was no.

I turned off the computer, lay down on the sofa under the window, and closed my eyes. Random thoughts started flooding into my head: How am I going to take care of the kids by myself? What is going to happen with our business that Mark handled? How can he really be gone? Twenty-four hours ago I thought he was alive.

This is the first morning without him in almost nine years. Where are you, Mark? Why did you die? Why?

There had to be a reason. I believed that, ever since Jean had died. I believed.

After Jean, Mark's stepmom, had died, I was wandering around a bookstore and stumbled onto a book called *Home with God*. It was written by Neale Donald Walsch, and was about near-death experiences and the possibilities of what may happen when a person dies. I thought it might be an interesting read and could offer a little perspective on what I was experiencing with Jean's presence.

That night as I lay in bed reading, I came across a section of the book that said we as humans with a spirit have *complete* free will. It said that not only do we have the ability to choose what food we eat, what car we drive, and what house we live in, but we are even able to choose when we *die*.

I sat there in bed for a moment and thought about it. I remembered how calm, relaxed, and happy Jean seemed before she died and wondered if there might be something to the idea. But honestly, being able to choose when we die seemed a little far-fetched.

As I kept reading, the book explained that most people who are sixty or older have had at least one near-death experience. It went on to say that in the moment of their decision they are shown their past and possible future.

I thought, "Future . . . what does that mean?" The book went on to say that we are shown exactly what will happen if we choose to die or if we choose to stay alive.

Then the universe gives us the choice to stay in our body or leave it. I felt as though I was experiencing déjà vu as I read the words of the book.

I suddenly sat up in bed, looked over at Mark, and said, "You know what? This is amazing. I've had a near-death experience!"

Mark set his book down on his legs, took his glasses off, looked at me, and said, "What are you talking about?"

"Well, before I met you, I was driving on the freeway going about sixty-five miles an hour, and I ran over a piece of cardboard. When that happened, I lost control of my car; the wheels were not responding to my steering. I hit the cement wall in the center of the road and totaled my car."

"Yeah, now I remember. You told me that you knew you would be okay, even before you hit the wall."

"Yes! But I don't think I told you how bad the wreck really was. As I hit the wall, the airbag exploded in my face, and the car began to spin. I hit the wall a second time on the back side of the car. When I came to a stop, I was sitting in the fast lane in the dark. I couldn't open the door because the car was bent so badly. Instead I put the convertible top down and crawled out.

"About five cars stopped, and several people ran over to see if I was okay. They made me sit down and brought me blankets and ice. They couldn't believe I wasn't hurt. I only had a bruised knee from hitting the dash, and my chin was stinging from the chemicals in the airbag that got on my skin when it exploded in my face.

"Not only was my car totaled, but when the firefighters arrived, they looked at it and then looked at me and one of them said, 'Are you the driver?' I said I was.

He shook his head and then said, 'There was an accident right here four days ago and the car didn't look that bad and it was a fatality.' The firemen were shocked that I didn't even need to go to the hospital to be checked for injuries."

Mark said, "I didn't realize it was that bad of an accident. You never really explained that part."

"I know, it never seemed that relevant until now. But here's the thing: I knew I would be okay because as my car was careening toward the cement wall, I heard in my head, 'Is this it?' and then I heard a very certain and resounding, 'NO!'

"At the time of the accident and up until just now, I thought that I was asking the universe if I was going to die and was then *told* 'No.' But I am starting to believe that isn't exactly what happened."

Mark's eyebrows were up, and I could tell he felt a little strange about what I was saying. But I kept on. "I think I was being *asked* if it was my time to go and that *I* was the one to say 'No!'

"When I look back at the whole experience, this new insight puts it into perspective. I remember seeing this flash of my past and a future with kids, and I knew that I wanted that more than anything, so I screamed 'No!'"

Mark's eyes softened. He must have realized I had not only chosen a longer life; I had also chosen a life with him. I said, "I knew without a doubt that it was not my time to go. I knew I wanted to stay and live more of my life. I was the one who chose that. I know it!"

Then I asked him, "Do you think Jean had the same information and chose to leave for a reason? Do you think that possibly everyone has that choice?"

"Well, I guess anything is possible. If that's what hap-pened to you, there must be some truth in it."

I leaned over and cuddled up in his arms. I lay there for a long time just listening to his heart and our breath-ing. Life felt a little more alive; and at the same time somehow it also felt a bit safer.

Suddenly the idea that we could actually choose our destiny was no longer a comfort. If Mark really had this power, he must have *chosen* to die.

But *why* would Mark have left us? The anger welled up in me like bile. I sat up and pushed my palms into the sides of my head. There was *no reason* he had to go right now! *None!* He was happy with his work, our marriage was very strong and getting better every day, he adored the boys, and he simply loved his life! His decision to die was so, so wrong. For the next three hours, anger ate at my soul.

SAM 'N DALLAS

After breakfast the next morning, the doorbell rang. I walked over, looked out the window, and saw Sam. He was facing my neighbor's house across the street. It felt like he couldn't face me and what had happened.

All of the anger I'd been wallowing in instantly melted away. Sam. He stepped in and put his arms around me, feeling smaller than I remembered. He also felt sad and weak and tired.

Sam had been Mark's college roommate and hunting buddy for thirty years. Normally he was not weak, but today he was. He let go of me and said, "Jen, I'm so sorry. What can I do?"

"Nothing. You're here. That's what matters."

"No, there are a lot of things that have to be done; there are a lot of people coming today. What can I do?"

I realized then that Sam needed to be moving and helping; he had to do something in order to survive this. I sat down at the kitchen table and made a list of things that needed to be done, both around the house and for people who were coming. Sam brightened when I handed him the list.

Then he said, "Where's Dallas?"

Sam and our ten-year-old chocolate Labrador, Dallas, were pretty close. I pointed to the back yard and he went outside. A few minutes later, he came back in holding a mangled piece of metal that vaguely looked like the downspout from our gutter.

He said, "I think Dallas did this."

So . . . she did know. I'd wondered how Dallas was going to react to Mark being gone. Now I knew.

She had been Mark's dog before I met him. The first night I went to his house for dinner and met her, she made her place known. As I was leaving, Mark came over to give me a hug, and Dallas promptly pushed her nose, then her whole body between us. I respected her for that move. We'd always had a great relationship since that night.

I looked up at Sam. "Is that our gutter?"

"Yes, and not only that; there are probably over a hundred pieces just like this scattered all over the yard."

"Is she okay? Is her mouth bleeding or anything?"

"No, she doesn't look hurt. I'll figure out how to get this fixed. Don't worry about anything. I'll also hang out with Dallas a lot today to make sure she is doing okay."

I was so relieved that I didn't have to handle Dallas, too. I wondered how I was going to manage everything else. I didn't have long to wonder; within an hour my dad and brother walked in the door.

How did Jeremy get here so fast? I wondered, as tears of joy came streaming out of my eyes. There weren't any flights from California this early.

My brother and I were extremely close but had not lived near each other in years. I missed him dearly, so seeing him suddenly and without notice was a treat like no other.

Then it hit me all over again: He was here because Mark had died. While this was going through my mind, Jeremy was walking over and taking me in his arms.

"How did you get here this early?" I asked.

"I got in late last night but didn't want to bother you. I'm sure you were exhausted."

"I'm so glad you're here."

"Me too. I'm so sorry." His voice cracked as he said it. Then he whispered in my ear, "I just always think of him calling me out of the blue like he used to and saying, 'Hey there, brother man!' I can't believe he is gone."

Jeremy's presence and those words sent a current of pain through my heart. They were brothers; Jeremy had lost his brother. We stood there holding each other with tears streaming out of our eyes and falling off our chins.

My dad had sat down at the table and was shuffling through some papers. He said, "Jen, I know this is hard, but we have to make some decisions, and we need your input."

A LIFE FULL OF LOVE

My stomach tightened a little when my Dad mentioned decisions. He said, "We have to decide on a funeral home and a place for a service, and I need to know if you want to bury him or not."

I took a deep breath and put my hands on my stomach. I knew my Dad was trying to be helpful, and I was so grateful that he was handling those things, but each word was like a one-two punch to my gut and face. I didn't know what Mark wanted. I didn't know what to do. I didn't feel as if I could make decisions about those things; I wasn't sure if I was even the one who should.

The phone rang and my mom picked it up—I still couldn't get myself to answer the phone, mainly because I still had the illogical, knee-jerk reaction that somehow it would be Mark calling, and when I answered I would get upset that it wasn't him. Not only that, but the phone seemed to be ringing all the time.

When Mom hung up she said, "That was Ray; he and Kathy and Karen are almost here. They wanted to make sure it was okay to come over. I told them it was."

I nodded at her. But how was I going to face Mark's dad? I looked up at my father and remembered he was there to get some information. I asked him how long I had to make the decisions.

"Today, preferably this morning," he said. "We have a lot of things we have to get done, and there is only today and tomorrow and then it will be the weekend."

I told him I wanted to talk to Mark's family; I thought they should have a say in these decisions, but I would make sure they were made as early as possible. Dad told me that he and Jeremy were going to try to handle as much of everything as they could, and he asked me what I wanted them to do the most.

"Handle everything about Mark. I don't think I can."

"Okay, I'll make every decision and do everything I can, and only bring you in for what I'm unable to do."

"Thank you."

I started to get up from the table and heard someone coming in the front door. It was Ray, Mark's dad. My body started to move toward him, and as it did everything in my vision blurred except for his eyes. When I got to him, I closed my eyes and almost fell into his arms. He held me and said, "It's going to be okay. We're here to take care of you. Don't worry. Everything is going to be alright."

I was scared to open my eyes; I knew I would see Mark. He and his dad had the same gentle eyes. I couldn't do it. Ray's loss was, in a very real way, worse than mine. His son wasn't supposed to go before he did. That wasn't the way nature intended it.

As Ray held me, a tangle of memories swirled uncontrollably in my mind: Mark and his Dad talking, sharing, hugging, smiling, and being together so completely. My two gentle souls who cherished each other were separated. As bad as my grief was, I couldn't even imagine Ray's.

I knew I was going to have to let go of Ray at some point, but I couldn't bring myself to. Mark was six feet five inches tall; his dad was even taller. Nobody ever held me like Mark did, and nobody else felt anything like Mark—except his dad. The warmth washed over me at the same time as the pain.

Then out of the corner of my eye I saw Mark's sisters. They were holding hands, watching us, and silently crying. They adored their brother, idolized him. He was their only brother, the glue in their family, and their little brother. I finally let go of Ray and walked over to them. We held each other, there in the entry way, until we could finally speak.

"Come in the dining room," I said. "I'm sorry to do this to you now, but I need some help."

We sat down at the table with my dad. I said, "Dad, I think I need them to help me with the decisions."

He looked over at them a little hesitantly. I know he must have felt horrible even bringing up the topics we were about to discuss. I'm sure he was imagining what it would be like if it were his son we were having to bury. He put his head down and said, "The first thing we have to decide is if he is going to be buried or cremated."

And there it was.

"We have to make that decision relatively soon, because if we want to bury him and have an open casket, they have to start to work on him."

God, was this conversation real?

I looked over at Mark's dad and sisters. Knowing I was going to get really upset, I stood and said, "I don't know what Mark wanted. I think this should be your decision. I have to go take a shower. Whatever you decide, I am okay with."

They looked at me, and I said, "Okay?"

They nodded their heads.

I went upstairs. When I got in the shower I realized it was the first one I'd taken since Mark was gone. It seemed that *every* single thing I did that was a first, I compared to how it had been when he was there. Even something as simple as taking a shower felt empty. Knowing there wasn't another adult in the world now who felt free to come in the bathroom while I was taking a shower felt like an aching void.

After I got dressed I went back downstairs. Everyone was still sitting at the table. A few of my neighbors were also in the kitchen, talking. I sat at the table, and one of Mark's sisters said, "Jen, we think Mark should be cremated. We talked about it, and he hated chemicals. He cared about the environment and nature, and we think he would have wanted that. What do you think?"

It made perfect sense. I said, "You're right. Dad, what else do you need?"

"You need to decide where you want to have the memorial service."

I knew a church was wrong, and a cemetery was wrong; Mark wouldn't have wanted either one. I wanted everything on that day to reflect the man he truly was.

One of my neighbors who was in the kitchen said, "Sorry to interrupt, but I was listening to what you were saying, and I had a thought. Why don't you have it at The Nature Center?"

The Nature Center wasn't far from our house. Later I could take the boys there to remember their dad. It was a place that shared information about local plants and animals, and it was absolutely beautiful. I thought it was a good idea.

Later that day we went to look over the facility. I knew having the service there was a good idea, but I didn't have the energy to work out the details. When we met with the person who would be handling the logistics, he said his name was Wade. That was my brother's middle name, and I felt this was a sign that we were in the right place. I said, "This place looks perfect. Dad, will you take care of this?"

"Yes."

When we got home, Jeremy asked if he could talk with me in private. We went upstairs to my office and he pulled out a catalog.

He said, "We need to choose an urn. Dad and I didn't think we should be the ones to do it."

When I thought about Mark's urn, I thought about his body disappearing. I thought about his face and his hands. Then it struck me: Mark had his wedding ring on when they took him.

"Do you know where Mark's wedding ring is?" I said.

Jeremy didn't move. I saw his brow start to furrow. Then he put his hands on his forehead and tears started streaming down his face. I didn't know what to do.

Without looking at me, he slowly reached in his shirt pocket and pulled out the ring. He held it in his palm for a moment and then handed it to me. When he could speak, he said, "They gave it to me when we were at the funeral home, but I just didn't know how to bring it up to you."

I took the ring and felt the weight of it in my hand. I never thought there would come a day when I would see it off of Mark's finger forever. The day we got married the crowd had laughed when I had trouble putting it on him. It was a little tight and the implications were perfect. I knew Mark never wanted to take the ring off. But now it was.

I folded my hand around it, sat there for a few minutes with Jeremy's warm body touching the right side of mine, and thought, "How is it really possible he's gone?"

That night I asked my Mom if she would sleep in my bed with me again. I woke up several times throughout the night with my heart and head racing. At four I woke up and had an overwhelming urge to go into my office and write. I hoped this was not going to be the new time I woke up every morning.

I got a pad of paper and a pen and sat down on the couch. I started to write about Mark and the way he lived his life. What came out of my mind was a list of ten traits or beliefs that Mark held and demonstrated. They must have been sitting right there in my heart, because they flowed out of me in about fifteen minutes. I never edited them.

A Life Full of Love

1. Smile and wave at your neighbors. – Be Neighborly.
2. Learn everyone's name and use it. – Be Friendly.
3. Give openly and with your heart. – Be Generous.
4. Hold hands. – Be Loving.
5. Laugh and be silly. – Be Happy.
6. Touch each other. – Be Gentle.
7. Don't marry the one you can live with, marry the one you can't live without. – Be true to yourself.
8. Never say or do anything you wouldn't want on the front page of the newspaper. – Be honest and live with integrity.
9. Go outside and play. – Be part of nature.
10. Say "I Love You" often.

I finished writing, and then I read through the list again. They were aspects of Mark that left an impression on others, the parts of him that he naturally demonstrated. While each of the traits was simple, his consistent use of them made him an extraordinary man. I wondered if maybe there was some way I could keep his influence alive.

REALITY

By the time the sun came up later that Friday morning, I'd slept a total of maybe five hours, and they had been restless hours, at that. Even within my exhaustion I wanted to know that my life might be okay at some point; I needed to do something that felt like me. I realized I had to get in the pool.

Swimming had been in my life for as long as I could remember. It had brought me joy, and it was a compass that kept me moving forward. A shining moment flashed into my head.

February 1988
Everything looked a bit blurry through my goggles. I could hear the water rushing past my ears but nothing else. Time seemed to slow down to a crawl. It was as if I were on autopilot.

I looked at the black line below me—still in silence except for the water. Then I turned my head to take a breath and heard the echoing roar of the crowd's screams inside the swim center.

I got a glimpse of my coach pumping his hands

over his head. My lungs freshly filled with new oxygen, I turned my face back down in the water. There were only about fifteen yards left in the race, but I wasn't tired. I wasn't running out of oxygen; I was on such a high that there was a calm in my body even though I knew I was swimming faster than I ever had.

I kicked my legs furiously but the burn still didn't come to my muscles. As I turned my head for my last breath before my final push to the wall, I saw my coach again and knew I was heading for a fantastic swim. His eyes were excited, and he was jumping up and down yelling with his arms in the air. I buried my head and swam the last few yards as hard as I could, but somehow it seemed just as easy as the beginning of the race.

When my fingertips hit the wall I pulled my body to the side, took a deep breath, yanked my goggles off, and looked up at the results on the clock. I put my face down into the water and smiled so hard I thought my cheeks would cramp. I'd done it! I had swum my fastest race ever.

I pulled myself out of the pool, peeled off my swim cap, grabbed my towel, and walked over to my coach. He looked at me, put his arms out to hug me, and said, "Nice job for a freshman!" I just smiled.

My coach let go of me and said, "I'm not sure if you realize it, Jennifer, but you have just qualified for three national swim meets."

I looked at him questioningly. I knew I'd swum fast enough to make the qualifying time to swim in the NCAAs, but I didn't know what else he was talking about.

"What do you mean?"

"You just qualified for the Senior Nationals, NCAAs, and Olympic Trials this summer."

I stood there in shock for a few seconds. I couldn't believe it. "Really?"

He nodded. "Warm down and we'll talk."

I went over to the warm-down pool and jumped in. I swam a few laps, got out, wiped my face with my towel, and climbed the stairs up to my parents in the stands.

As soon as I got within reach, they grabbed me and hugged me. "That was fantastic, Jennifer! That was your best time, right?"

"Yes, and that's not all. I qualified for the Senior Nationals, NCAAs, and Olympic Trials. I'm pretty sure I'll be going to Texas, Indianapolis, and Florida this summer!"

They looked happy, but I detected a little worry. I knew they were concerned that it would cost a lot of money, so I said, "Don't worry, the school pays for everything. As a matter of fact, with that swim, they will probably be paying for a lot more things in the future."

As it turned out, my prediction came true. Over the next three years I ate, slept, and breathed swimming even more than I had the previous twelve. I swam, lifted weights, and trained for more hours than I spent in the classroom. Swimming essentially became my entire life.

I felt that I needed to reconnect with something that felt normal—that I should go swim. At the same time, it felt as if swimming would be *too* normal. I worried that if I went to the pool by myself that I might end up crying the whole time, and that wasn't why I wanted to go. I called my brother who was staying over at my dad's house.

"Hey, Sis."

God, even *that* felt a little bit normal, I realized.

I said, "I'm thinking of going for a swim, but I don't think I can go by myself. Did you bring your suit?"

"Sure did. I thought it might be a good idea."

I was so relieved. It had been years since I had swum with my brother. We trained in the same pool for twelve years as kids but had let that part of our lives split during adulthood.

He picked me up and we drove to the pool; my dad came too. As we walked in I saw my two best swim buddies hanging on the gutter, laughing. I was scared that when they saw me they would stop laughing. That would be too much; I didn't want to be *that* person, a downer in people's lives.

I walked over and said, "Hey! How's the water?"

They looked up, smiled, and said, "Great!"

Thank God!

The pool was crystal clear. The sun reflected sharply off the water, but it was still quite cool outside. It was the kind of morning that made you want to run and dive in as soon as you took your clothes off. So I did.

As my fingertips hit the water and the rest of my body slid in, I felt the exhilaration of going from the lightness of air to the more fluid solidity of water. In that moment a little tiny bit of the joy that was buried under the pain in my heart squeezed through from out of the darkness. The child in me peeked out from behind the mountain of grief and smiled. The pool had always been an integral part of my sanity, and today was no exception.

That morning my brother told me he had not swum a real work-out in about five years. We swam past our dad several times, giving him a little ribbing for being slow. We did a few intervals with my friends. I think they may have let me beat them, but it didn't matter. All that mattered was I'd found a tiny glimmer of light that I knew I'd be able to make brighter each day. The water had a power over me, over our whole family. With an ache in my heart I thought about the trip Mark and I had planned with the boys to Cozumel— the trip that would never be what we had intended.

PUBLIC

I ate a little breakfast and then asked my mom to go with me to a jewelry store so I could get a chain to wear Mark's wedding ring around my neck. She agreed and also suggested we stop by the grocery store to order a cake for the kids "party" after the service on Monday.

Going to the grocery store was too much for me, as it turned out. I saw neighbors who couldn't look me straight in the eye, but the hardest thing for me to handle was seeing fathers with their children. I broke down. Mom managed to order the cake and helped me get to the car. I sat there crying for a few minutes. How was I going to live a normal life and do everything I needed to do for the boys if I couldn't even go to the grocery store?

When I stopped crying, my mom asked me if I still wanted to go to the jewelry store. I said I did.

For some reason, I felt like I *had* to get a chain. I'd been holding Mark's ring in my hand; I wanted it with me always. I couldn't just hold it, and I didn't want to lose it. I thought that maybe wearing it around my neck would give me strength.

As we went into the store, I worried that I might get upset again, but some of my will to keep moving came back. We asked the man at the counter to show us some chains that could hold the ring. There were several different chains to choose from, but I didn't like any of them very much.

There was one design that would hold the weight of the ring that I liked a little. It came in two lengths: one was shorter, about the length of a choker, and one was longer. I looked at them both for a minute but couldn't decide which one to get. I didn't want to leave the store and have to go somewhere else.

I felt as though I needed help in making the decision, but for some reason my mom was not the right one to help. I told her I needed a minute by myself. I could tell by the look on her face that she was a little worried to leave my side after the episode at the grocery store, but I knew I'd be okay.

I turned away from her and walked to the other side of the store and took a few slow breaths. Then I felt the urge to look to the left. The instant I looked into a jewelry case I felt guilty. Mark had died just two days ago and I was thinking about jewelry?

However in the same instant the feeling of guilt hit me, I heard—or maybe thought—"Quit looking; you will have plenty of time for that later."

The words were spoken in a joking tone. I looked around the store. There wasn't anyone near me. I knew Mark would have said something like that, but he wasn't there. Was he?

I felt a warmth flow through my heart. I took my first full deep breath in two days, smiled a little, and laughed inside. Next I heard, "You need to get the long chain."

I turned around and walked back to the counter, we bought the longer chain, and we went home.

In the afternoon I asked my mom if she would go to Cozumel with me and the boys. It seemed too difficult to face staying home. As I was talking with her, I suddenly realized that Mark and I were supposed to go get the boys' passports in the afternoon on the day he had died.

A feeling of dread landed on me when I remembered what Mark had told me at lunch on Tuesday: In order to get the passports in time for the trip, he and I *both* needed to be at the appointment to expedite them. I knew there was no way I would even have a death certificate in time to get the boys their passports.

I looked up at my mom and said, "There is no way we can go. The boys don't have their passports."

"Oh, Jen. I'm so sorry."

I didn't think I could make the call to cancel our reservations, so I asked her to handle it. She nodded and went to get the information off my computer to make the call.

A little while later my brother and dad walked into the house. They both looked exhausted. I realized they had probably been staying up late talking as well as handling all of the details all day long for the funeral home and the service on Monday.

My brother slumped down in the chair next to me. I wasn't sure I'd ever seen him look so tired.

He said, "Jen, I can handle everything else, but I just don't know how to figure out how much food to order."

But the unspoken message I heard was, "Help me, I'm drowning. This is the last straw."

Even though he would never say those words, I knew I needed to get him and my dad some help. I closed my eyes for a minute and thought, "Who can help them?"

For some reason the face of my neighbor Alissa popped into my head. She wasn't a caterer or anything, but she did like to cook. I thought maybe she could help him with deciding about the food.

I gave her number to my brother, and he called her. Within moments I saw relief on his face. She must have said she would help.

That night after dinner I was sitting around the table with the boys, and I was wearing the chain with Mark's ring around my neck. The shirt I was wearing was low enough to show the ring. Brannon got off his chair, came over, crawled up on my lap, and sat there facing me. He smiled up at me and then he noticed the ring. He took it in his tiny hand and started to turn it around in his little fingers.

An image flashed into my head of when I would read to him before bed. He had a habit of holding my finger and turning my ring around in his fingers like he was doing now with Mark's.

While I started to wonder if he also did that with Mark's ring, Brannon's lower lip began to tremble. Within moments a flood of tears and cries started. He could not verbalize his feelings through words as an adult could, but he did not have to.

For the next two hours he was completely inconsolable. He cried nonstop, even though I held him, rocked him, stroked his hair, and carried him around whispering gently in his ear that everything would be okay.

During those two hours I realized there was a purpose to the longer chain. It was meant to hide the ring under my shirts. I could still wear the ring and it would comfort me, but it would not cause pain for the boys.

THE GIFT

On Friday night I decided to sleep in the guest room by myself. I hadn't had any luck sleeping in our bed, even with someone there. I thought maybe I needed some distance from my bed and some time alone. I knew for sure I needed some sleep; I was becoming a walking zombie.

I went into the guest bedroom and looked at the bed. It wasn't usually mine, but it was tonight. I crawled in bed and for the first time since the early morning of that day, realized I was alone. All of the stress and emotions of the last three days rushed into me and I began to sob.

I was surprised that I had any tears left. But these felt different; they were mixed with feelings of letting go. I was starting to believe Mark was gone. There seemed to be a release and an acceptance that was settling into my body.

As my mind broke into surrender, I tried to fathom our new life. But all I could think was, "How are the boys going to make it through this without huge, lifelong wounds?"

They were *so* close to Mark. I couldn't understand why this had happened. With these thoughts, anger began to well up, along with the acceptance. It became so strong that it started to win and push the acceptance out of me.

All I could think was that Mark's death was so wrong and unfair, and that the timing was horrible. For the last two days I'd been having an ongoing struggle in the back of my mind. I wanted to believe that everyone had ultimate free will to decide when they die. But if that were true, then Mark *never* would have left. It just couldn't be true that it was his choice. It wasn't right!

Either I was off-base with reality, or maybe—just maybe—there was a reason.

But there *couldn't* be a reason!

The conflict had been sitting there like a hot stone under the ashes of my grief, constantly burning me.

We had two young children who Mark adored; we were happy in our marriage; he loved his work; he absolutely loved his life. Death couldn't possibly have been his will. Why in the world would he have *chosen* to leave us when the boys were so young? The anger was blinding.

I laid there screaming in my head, "Why? Why? Why?"

Through the cloud of screaming came a voice like a soft breath of wind that cleared the fog. It said, "Do you really want to know?"

I stopped breathing; my body slammed to a halt and became instantly and fully alert.

There was nobody in the room with me. I did *not* say that!

Then my brain clicked in for a second and I realized what had been said: "Do you really want to know?"

I didn't say or think anything. My mind was a clear, clean slate. My heart was paralyzed with fearful hope that there could be an answer at all, much less that I would know what it was. And then there were only six simply stated words . . .

"Brannon would have *drowned* in Cozumel."

WHAT? WHAT? NO!!! My thoughts stopped. My body convulsed into a fetal position and the tears came like waves. I was hit with so many emotions all at once: frustration, relief, understanding, disbelief, anger, sadness . . . I felt sick.

At some point a moment came when I thought, "There is no way Brannon would have drowned! *My children do not drown.*"

I couldn't even imagine it. He'd been in private swim lessons for months. But even so, there was a small pain in my heart, a thought tugging at me that was saying, "God, what if it's true? What if we would have lost Brannon?"

I lay there struggling with the information. Still facing the dark horror of losing Mark, I now had a tiny glimmer of something else. Knowing that there really was a reason was a *comfort* like no other. But that night the two feelings—horror and comfort—would not fit into my body together. After what seemed like days of struggle, I drifted off to sleep and slept soundly until the morning.

BELIEVE

When I woke up, the words were still ringing in my mind: "Brannon would have drowned in Cozumel." I was still pondering them when I went downstairs to the kitchen.

Then I heard Brannon's bedroom door open. I couldn't wait to see him. I was sitting at the kitchen table talking with my mom, but I stood up mid-sentence and walked toward the bottom of the stairs. When he saw me, his deep brown eyes looked into mine, and I sensed a connection. Was it possible that somewhere, somehow, our spirits knew the truth?

When we got to each other, he opened his arms to hug me as I was kneeling down to him. I took him in my arms and held him as close to my heart as I could. We were holding each other; we were together. Nothing else in the world mattered in that moment.

~

Later in the morning I was at the hairdresser with my mom. Even though it felt silly, I wanted to look nice for Mark at the memorial service on Monday.

My mom had missed her haircut appointment in California

when she left so quickly on Wednesday, so she came with me and got hers cut as well.

I was debating whether or not to tell her about what I had heard the night before. As far as I knew, she had never believed in the afterlife or spirituality. It wasn't something we talked about when I was growing up.

I knew at some point I would have to tell *someone*, and I thought that Mom might be the safest one to tell first. After all, she was my mom; if she thought I was going crazy, she would tell me. Besides, Mark's voice had given me some peace, and I hoped that it would give her some peace as well.

We were sitting on a couch waiting for the hairdresser and I decided to tell her. I took a deep breath. "Mom, I need to tell you something."

"Okay, what is it?"

I knew she wasn't really prepared for what I was about to say, but I also knew that maybe preparation for the information wasn't possible.

"Mark spoke with me last night."

Her eyes opened a tiny bit, but she didn't say anything.

"He told me that if he would have stayed alive that Brannon would have drowned in Cozumel."

Her mouth dropped open and her face seemed to slump. Huge tears immediately began to fall from her eyes and she started to shake. I put my hand on her leg to steady her and moved next to her to hold her. I knew what she was going through; if she believed it at all, then she was in shock, as I'd been the night before.

I couldn't remember ever seeing my mother cry. It struck me that maybe she *did* believe me. It also struck me that she of all people would understand that it was not something I could have made up. She was with me during my childhood at all of the swim meets.

She probably couldn't imagine her grandchildren drowning, just as I couldn't imagine my children drowning.

When she could speak, she said softly in my ear, "It makes perfect sense. That sounds exactly like Mark."

I was so relieved that she understood and didn't think I was crazy. I was also relieved because even though she was crying and obviously shaken, her shoulders had relaxed a little and she looked more at peace.

When we walked in the door after coming home from the hair salon, the phone was ringing. I went to pick it up for the first time since Mark had died; I wasn't afraid of the ringtone anymore.

It was Alissa. She had a question about the food for the service. She wanted to clarify exactly what I wanted to order. During the conversation she laughed and said, "I have to tell you something."

I wondered what it was.

She said, "I got married at The Nature Center. Not only that, we used the same restaurant you're using for the memorial to cater our rehearsal dinner."

I sat there and didn't say a word. I had not known her when she was single, and I didn't realize she had gotten married at The Nature Center. The coincidences were a bit unnerving, though very welcome. She was going to be a huge help for Jeremy and Dad.

Throughout the day my mind wouldn't stop spinning. I kept thinking about Brannon being gone and Mark making the decision to go. At one point I realized with a jolt that had Mark been there for even *one* more day, we would have gotten the boys' passports. If we had, then there would have been a chance for us to go to Cozumel even though he had died.

THE FUTURE

When I went to bed that night I was still trying to wrap my head around Mark saying he had died to keep Brannon from drowning. A part of me felt relieved that there was a reason for Mark leaving, but I also felt a growing frustration. I had some serious questions.

If it was true that Brannon would have drowned in Cozumel, there *must* have been another way to stop it. Couldn't Mark have gone on a business trip? Lost the passports? Talked me out of the trip?

I started to get angry again. I began to yell in my head, "Couldn't there have been another way? What a joke! You didn't have to *die*! Isn't that a little extreme?"

Once again, out of the depths of my deep emptiness came his calm, warm, gentle voice: "No, that trip was going to be a huge step for our family. We had never gone on a vacation by ourselves before. If I had chosen to stay, we would have gone. We were too strong to let anything get in our way."

When I heard the words, I knew they were true. If I'd had their passports after Mark had died, I might have even taken the boys without him.

And then I heard, "And, if we would have gone, there would have been nothing we could have done to save Brannon. He would have drowned."

At that point I decided that if Mark was going to give me answers, then I was going to ask for more of them. I hesitantly thought, "Why . . . you? Why did *you* have to die? Why not Brannon?"

Even though I wasn't actually speaking, my throat closed in on itself. The thought I had just expressed was unimaginable. I began to understand just from asking the question why Mark made the choice he made.

Even so, there was his voice: "I left for *all* of you."

I was confused by his answer.

"Had I stayed, which I could have, Brannon would have drowned. When that happened, our lives would have been ripped to shreds. You would have felt so guilty, and I would have been so angry with you. I would have never forgiven you for losing Brannon. I would have blamed you completely for his death. You were the swimmer, and in my eyes it was your responsibility to make sure the boys were safe in the water."

It was strange for me to think about the full impact of Brannon being gone. I sat with what he said for a minute.

Then I heard, "We would have divorced."

Thoughts of denial flooded into my head. There was no way I would have let our marriage fall apart! Not after what we had accomplished together so far.

He must have heard that thought, because he said, "There would have been nothing you could have done. You were a competitive swimmer; if your child had died from drowning, *you* would have blamed yourself. And I, too, would have blamed you. Even if you had wanted the marriage to work, I would have left. You wouldn't have had a choice."

As I was trying to digest everything he was saying, he said, "And then there's Connor. Had he lost Brannon he would have been a different child. His whole life would have been shattered. They're so close and laugh so much—he would have stopped laughing.

Can you imagine Connor not laughing? Has he laughed with his brother in the last four days?"

I hated to admit it, but he had. Connor and Brannon together had obviously been sad at times, but they had definitely been acting like fairly normal kids. They played, laughed, ran around, and just enjoyed being with each other. They seemed to be taking care of each other. I tried to imagine Connor without Brannon. He would have been devastated.

Then I heard, "Not only would Connor have changed dramatically from losing Brannon, but he would have witnessed our love turn to hate. This would have been like ripping what was left of his foundation out from under him. He would have felt completely alone, as if he had no control over his life."

And finally, as if it wasn't enough information for me to digest already, he said, "I wouldn't have been able to bear the pain, guilt, and loneliness of my life. I would have hated myself for destroying your life and Connor's. I'd have chosen to die after our divorce.

"Worst of all, Connor's will to live would have been completely destroyed. He would not have allowed himself to live a full life. He'd have thought that his dad and brother didn't get to live, so why should he?"

Those words were like hard blows to my body. I was unable to imagine anything that Mark and I couldn't work through. We'd been through layoffs, deaths, sicknesses, business strains, building a home, and much more. I just couldn't imagine us not working it out.

On the other hand, I was also unable to comprehend losing Brannon and the effect that would have had on our marriage and on Connor.

The last thing I heard was, "I left for all of you."

The next morning Connor and Brannon came downstairs looking for me. When they walked into the kitchen together, the conversation from last night flooded into my head. However unreal it seemed, the reality was that the three of us were here together. In addition, even without Mark, now I knew this alternative was better than the other.

I realized as I watched them together that I did not pity them any longer. Instead, I was grateful for their existence. I walked over and took them in my arms and thought, "You two are the luckiest boys in the entire world."

They *were* lucky. They were loved, and they were alive. That was what mattered. The world felt bright and clear. What was happening with us was what was supposed to be happening. I was so grateful I couldn't speak. I did, however, hold them in my arms for as long as they would let me.

BUSINESS

I sat down with my brother at breakfast and asked him where we were on the details about the service and putting the program together. While we were trying to think of someone who could help, my sister-in-law came in and asked what we were talking about, and we told her.

She grinned and said, "I'll do the program."

My brother and I looked at each other, feeling like idiots. It was so obvious! She was a designer and an artist and could definitely put together a program.

"That would be great," I told her.

She went up to my office and started on it.

Later that day, Sabrina, the marriage counselor Mark and I had been seeing, came over to the house. She wanted to talk with me about the cycles of grief and healing that the boys and I were probably in the process of experiencing.

When she walked in, I looked at her and wondered if she might be willing to be the speaker at Mark's memorial service. I didn't know if she had ever done anything like it before, but I asked anyway.

"Of course I will," she said. "Actually I thought of it a couple of days ago but didn't want to be presumptuous. I've never done a memorial service before, but I'd be honored. Plus, I told Mark I had his back covered, remember?"

One month ago.

In January our counseling was going so well that one day during a session Sabrina said, "You know, I think you guys will be done with this soon."

Mark looked up at her, grinned, and said, "But don't you think we need to come in periodically for tune-ups?"

He had begun to like our sessions and our home-work, realizing how fantastic our marriage was becoming as a result of the effort. As we were holding hands and walking out the door from what would be—though we didn't know it then—our last session together, he looked over his shoulder at Sabrina, pointed at me, and very jokingly said, "Think we can take care of *her* now?"

Sabrina grinned and said, "Don't worry; I've got your back."

I was so happy. I ran upstairs and made a copy of the ten things I'd written about Mark. I told her I wanted to use the ten aspects that Mark lived by as an outline for the service, and I wanted her to invite his friends and family to speak about him after each subject.

Later that night I set up a meeting with the financial partners Mark and I had for our business. I had some major concerns now that Mark wasn't around to handle the daily business: I didn't know how to run the day-to-day aspects of the company, nor did I really want to learn. I knew that if I was going to be able to keep it running, I was going to have to hire someone.

I thought back to when Mark had decided to work with our partners and wondered how I should handle the meeting.

January 2004

When Connor was four months old, Mark came home from work early with a big box in his arms.

"What is that?" I asked him.

He looked at me with a sadness in his eyes that I'd never seen and said, "I was laid off."

I couldn't believe my ears. My instant thought was, "We have a four-month-old and I'm not working. What are we going to do?" Then the very next thought put a smile on my face, and I shared it with Mark.

"Sweetie, that's great! We'll be fine. We have some savings. Now you can go out on your own. I'm so happy!"

He didn't seem so sure. He had worked in the same business for twenty-five years and had always been the one to get promoted and headhunted out of companies by competitors. Being out of work was new for him. I knew he felt like a failure, but I wasn't going to let him feel that way for long.

After a couple of days of licking his wounds, he picked up the phone and talked with several people who could be our partners. I asked him who he thought would work out the best.

"The Athens Group."

"Are you sure?"

"Yes, I've known the owners for twenty years, and

I worked with them off and on for ten. They would be trustworthy with just a handshake on a million-dollar deal. There isn't anyone else I'd want to work with at this point."

I smiled at him and said, "Okay, let me know how the meeting goes."

Within two days Mark had cemented a deal with them to be our financial partners. He started working with fervor to get customers to use him as their supplier.

Over the next three years we rode the rollercoaster of a new business, experiencing highs when things went our way and deep lows when the reality of tight market competition reared its head. However, throughout all of it, the one thing I noticed was that Mark seemed more alive. When he was working, he was passionate about his work. When he wasn't working, he was more passionate about life. And, he always trusted our partners.

When Mark and I had first started the company, I asked him what I should do if anything ever happened to him. The only thing I remembered him saying was, "Call Randy."

I'd approached Randy about working with our company on Friday, but he said he couldn't. He even said that Mark had called him the day before he died. I remembered overhearing the conversation before we left for lunch.

"Randy," Mark said, "when are you going to quit that dead end job and come work with me?"

I had stood there for a minute, smiling. Mark had always wanted to have Randy come work in our business.

But on Friday Randy told me his wife was newly pregnant and

that he was really happy in his current job. I understood his reasoning but didn't know what to do. Randy said he would help me hire someone who was familiar with our industry. I said okay, but for some reason it just didn't feel right.

Randy had reminded me that their friend David, who had been a groomsman in our wedding, had done the same job as Mark had when they worked in the past together. Even though David could have handled the job, I didn't seriously consider him as a candidate because he was now a full time real estate agent like me. He'd been active in real estate and had participated on my investing team for a couple of years.

I was very nervous about meeting with our financial partners. I had only met one of the owners; Mark had always been the one to communicate with them. I asked Randy if he would come to the meeting at our house, and he agreed.

I also asked my dad, stepdad, and brother to come to help make decisions. My brother decided not to come because the meeting was at night, he was exhausted, and his wife and two small boys needed him. I told him it was fine, since I had three other people there to listen and help.

At the meeting our partners said that if I wanted, they could take over the part of the business that Mark was handling. I had wondered if that was what they were going to offer; I knew it was an option and not a bad one.

The only problem was that I wanted the company to be there for our boys to step into when they were old enough to work. I knew if I let our partners take over the business that most likely it would not be an option for Connor and Brannon in the future.

I told them I wanted to hire someone and continue running the business as Mark had. They looked relieved. *I* was relieved that *they* looked relieved, even though I knew this path would be much harder, especially in the short term, when I had to figure out how to manage without Mark and at the same time get someone trained.

We decided to start looking for someone to hire and closed the meeting. I said good night to everyone and went upstairs to get the boys ready for bed.

THE BATH

While I was giving the boys a bath, my college roommate and very dear friend Tab arrived from San Diego. When she walked into the bathroom, I was so happy to see her I jumped up and gave her a hug, even though I had bubbles up to my elbows.

We both sat on the floor while the boys splashed and laughed, and I quietly told her the story of what Mark had told me.

As I was talking she caught her breath and told me she had chills. We had been on the swim team together in college. Neither of us could imagine any of our children drowning.

I looked over at the boys who were playing and laughing with joy, only five days after their father had died. She looked at them too. We were silent for a few moments, and then I said, "Can you imagine Connor without Brannon?"

She shook her head; she was unable to speak.

I felt a sense of calm spread through the room. It was as if Mark was there with us, watching them too and feeling happy. I knew why he did what he did.

When I stood up to get the towels for the boys, I looked at the mirror and saw the note Mark had written to me from Brannon the night before he died, and for some reason I looked a little closer at it. I read it again and blinked but still couldn't believe my eyes.

I read it a third time and realized it really didn't say, "Smack! I love you, Brannon" as if Brannon was talking to me, but said instead, "Smack! I love you Brannon!"

The difference in punctuation was minimal, but the meaning was completely flipped. Had Mark specifically left Brannon a note telling him he loved him the night before he died? Somewhere deep down had he known he was going to go that night? I shook my head.

After the boys were in bed, Tab and I went downstairs and sat down on the couch in the living room. We began to talk about the last time she had visited, which was at our wedding.

She smiled and said, "Remember the night of your rehearsal dinner?"

It was a beautiful October night, but after dinner the wind started to blow and a monster storm came in. Mark didn't think much about the weather because he was raised where there were storms all the time, but Tab and I weren't, and we loved the excitement! She actually slept out on our deck on a hammock that night so she could watch the storm.

She pointed at the window and said, "Look."

I turned and saw a flash of lightning. A few seconds later there was a low rumble of thunder. We hadn't had rain in weeks, maybe even months. But that night there was a storm similar to the one the night before our wedding.

Tab asked me if I was going to speak at the service. I'd been struggling with the idea myself, and I told her I couldn't decide. I didn't know if I'd be able to talk in front of people without breaking down. I also didn't have anything prepared; nothing I could think of seemed right. Most people I had talked with said I didn't need to speak and that nobody expected me to.

Tab, on the other hand, simply said, "You should."

THE PAST

That night in bed more questions started to pop up in my mind. I wondered, "Did you die because of something I did? Did I push you too hard with the boys? With our marriage? With health issues?"

If I thought logically about the questions, they didn't make sense, but it didn't matter; they were in my head anyway. When I asked if anything I had done had pushed Mark to decide to die, I heard, "No."

I wanted to ask something more, but I didn't know what. Then he said, "I would have died seven years ago if I hadn't decided to marry you."

I heard the words he was saying, but they didn't make sense.

"What are you talking about?"

"Because of the changes you brought into my life, I lived longer. I've had this condition for years. My body was already starting to fail before I met you. You helped me stop drinking as much alcohol, eat healthier, and even exercise *less,* which ultimately kept me alive."

I wondered what he meant by "this condition" but then I kind of chuckled, because it seemed funny that *not* exercising would be helpful. I also thought, "I really wanted you to exercise more, but for some reason I never pushed it. If it somehow kept you alive longer, then I guess now I know there was a reason. Maybe somewhere deep down *I* knew."

Then I realized something: we got *married* seven years ago.

"Yes," he said, "I would have chosen to die on the day of our wedding. It was my alternate path had I not met you and decided to continue with you in my life."

These things I was hearing started to feel a bit unreal. He would have died if he hadn't married me? How was that possible? Wouldn't he have just been alone or with someone else? This was crazy! In a tiny moment of acceptance, however, it started to dawn on me how powerful we really are and how decisions we make on a daily basis really do affect the rest of our lives.

I was getting lost and tangled in the thoughts when I was jolted out of them by his next words.

"There's more. There was another time when I could have chosen to die."

I wasn't sure I wanted to hear what he was going to say, but I just waited.

"The day you walked over to Sabrina's house and asked her to help with our marriage . . . I had the choice to leave *that* night. When it hit me how much you cared about our marriage, it was impossible to leave."

I gripped my chest with my hands as the tears streamed from my eyes. I remembered that day as if it were yesterday.

I'd been a real estate agent for seventeen years and an investor for sixteen of those years. During 2008 I had done several real estate investments and was looking into buying a much larger property than I had ever owned. I felt strongly that my background had led me to this place in my career and prepared me for it. Mark didn't want to take the risk and told me so.

Over the next couple of months our arguments got louder. He felt I shouldn't buy any more real estate; I felt it was the natural progression of my career. The arguments became so frequent and loud that we even began fighting in front of the boys.

Four years prior, when Mark had been laid off and started our other business, I had supported him one hundred percent. I'd used all of my savings from before we were married to pay our bills, I had done all of the office work, and I'd propped him up emotionally when times were tough. I'd told him over and over I knew he would be a huge success.

Now it was my turn to have some success in my career and I wanted to have *his* support, but instead he was turning on me. It made me crazy! I thought I had the tools to deal with conflict like this, but it became too much.

One morning I was so distraught about our disagreements that I called my neighbor Sabrina, who was a counselor. She invited me to come over and talk. I hung up the phone, walked past Mark's office without a word, and went out the door to her house.

I told her that if things didn't get better there was no way I could stay. I didn't want to leave, but the arguing and yelling had gotten so bad that I felt the boys were being harmed, and I wouldn't do that to them anymore.

Sabrina listened to everything I had to say. Then she responded, "I watch you two with your kids playing out in the cul-de-sac, and you are both great with them. They deserve parents that can express themselves in ways that don't hurt their ears or their hearts.

"I'm happy to give you the names of some other counselors, or I'm happy to see you myself since we don't socialize and we're moving across town in about a month. Jennifer, I want you to know that if we work together I will consider myself to be working for your boys.

"I know that underneath all this disagreement you love each other, and with some effort you can shift your marriage from an invisible divorce to a conscious, compassionate relationship."

I knew counseling would not be an easy road. However I also knew the alternative was not what I truly wanted in my heart: I wanted our marriage back.

I walked back to our house and had to go by Mark's office on the way in. He looked up and said, "Why did you go to Sabrina's?"

I was scared to tell him because I thought he might get angry, but I decided he needed to know.

"I can't deal with the fighting anymore. It is hurting us and the boys. I have to do something. I'm going to counseling."

He looked me straight in the eyes and said without any hesitation, "If you're going to counseling, then I am too."

I nodded my head and went up to my office. I couldn't admit it right then, but there was a little slice of hope in my heart that was whispering to me that if he was also willing, then we could work it all out. But the last year had been so hard that I didn't want to be too hopeful.

I remembered the exact moment when I made the decision to go to Sabrina's house. The fear, hurt, and anger that were so present in my heart that day had begun to turn toward hope when I walked back in.

He said, "Yes, remember how I immediately said I would go, too?"

I did.

"Well, that night I would have died just like I did four days ago. My body was done, I had nothing left. I was fighting so hard in so many ways and it was finished. But you brought hope and light into my world that day, and I could not bear to leave. I had to see us get better. I knew in my heart we would, and I wanted the boys to witness us making it right. I pretty much lived on fumes for the nine months after that."

I thought about how far we'd come from the days of fighting and remembered our last date night a couple of weeks ago and how wonderful it had felt to really connect with him.

Dinner seemed to be going well; we'd been talking easily about everything. But then I brought up the list of things I'd given him that I wanted to do over the next year. I was excited to talk about our future together.

He instantly stiffened.

I couldn't understand why. But then he said, "I thought we weren't going to buy any more real estate."

I stopped moving. I had put on the list that I wanted to buy some investments, and now I was scared we were going to revert back into anger and fighting.

He went on about how he thought I was supposed to get the okay from him first. I tried to tell him that was why I wrote the list and why I wanted to talk about it, but he just got more frustrated.

I tried to sit there and not say anything for fear of saying something else to trigger his anger. He then got really quiet for about a minute.

When he finally spoke he said, "It made me sad when you said in our counseling session today that I say 'I love you' too much."

I was stunned.

I looked at him and said, "I'm so, so sorry. I didn't mean to make you sad. It isn't that you say it too much; it's just that when I hear it over and over I feel as if it isn't heartfelt, that it's just a habit. But I know that's my stupid issue, not yours. I don't want you to stop saying 'I love you.' I'm so sorry."

I felt like such a jerk.

He looked up at me, smiled gently, and said, "Thank you."

There was an instant release of pressure. He relaxed, and so did I. The rest of our evening was incredible. I almost couldn't believe how happy I was and how close I felt to him. I felt honored to be trusted with his vulnerable feelings and for him to know I had not intended to hurt him and would try my best to avoid hurting him.

I was having a hard time taking in everything he was saying, but he kept on going. "And we even did better than I expected; we made our lives bliss. Every day got better and better. And then when the time came again to choose to leave or not, it was *so* hard. I knew that this time, because of Brannon, there wasn't an option, but I did *not* want to leave you. I was so excited for our lives."

The tears were streaming down my face. I realized that he had held on for those nine months until the last moment he possibly could. I also remembered how he was when I found him four days ago. He was lying as if sleeping peacefully, except one of his eyes was open just a tiny bit. It made me wonder if he almost changed his mind at the last moment.

He said, "Yes, I almost didn't do it. I almost couldn't leave *you*."

The words were so true for me, too. I did *not* want him to go. The fact that he struggled with leaving was comforting, but at the same time a deep tightness gripped my chest, and I knew it would be a while before it would start to let go.

HEART

I woke up with a jolt and looked at the clock. It was almost 7:00 AM. The memorial was going to start in three hours—unbelievable! How was I going to possibly honor Mark's life in a way that would really do it justice?

I hadn't prepared anything to say, but for some reason I wasn't worried. I knew something would come to me when it was right, even if the moment was when I was already standing in front of everyone.

I went through the motions of getting ready to go. When I was in my closet deciding what to wear, I couldn't do it—I just couldn't wear black. Mark wasn't a dark person.

My clothes needed to somehow reflect that I wasn't in the dungeon anymore. The last three nights of talking with Mark had pulled me up far enough to stand up straight and look people in the eye without having grief be the only thing communicated between us.

I scanned my clothes. It was cold outside, so I didn't have that many things to choose from. After looking through my sweaters, I picked out a green one and some jeans. Green was Mark's favorite color. That seemed as good a reason as any to choose it.

After I got the boys fed and dressed, Cheryl arrived to watch them during the service and then bring them later for the "Celebration Party" with cake and a piñata (at their request). Sabrina and Lydia both had said that having the boys at the memorial service was not a good idea; I took their advice.

I had a few minutes to myself before I had to walk out the door, so I decided to see if I had any voice mail messages that needed attention.

There were messages from a couple of friends with condolences, and then I heard a voice I didn't recognize. It was the woman from the Medical Examiner's office who had performed the autopsy. The system indicated she had left the message late Friday, but for some reason I had not gotten the call.

She said, "Hi, Mrs. Hawkins. I am sorry to leave this in a message, but I figured you would want to know what happened as soon as possible. Your husband Mark died from natural causes. The autopsy showed he died from an enlarged heart."

My knees buckled, and I grabbed the counter to stop from falling. I felt crushed and relieved at the same time. An enlarged heart? Are you serious? Is that a real disease? Then finally, the thought came to me, "*Of course* he died from an enlarged heart." Mark had the biggest heart of anyone I knew.

I sat down on a chair by the kitchen table; I could barely hold the phone up to my ear, so I leaned into it instead. She continued on to say that it may have been a genetic issue, but there was no way to know for sure. She said I should call her for more information, because I might want to have the boys looked at by a doctor. I put my hand to my heart and listened for the boys playing in the other room. Dear God—No.

My thoughts started to spin. Mark had told me the other night that he had the condition for *years*. What if he did have a genetic defect? I wasn't sure I was strong enough to deal with this.

I realized she was still talking, saying that Mark had several signs of a genetic problem called Marfan's Syndrome. She said his height of six feet five inches was a sign, as were his long arms; that his joints were more flexible than normal; and on and on. I didn't really hear anything else because my brain stopped taking in information when she mentioned the boys.

I hung up and decided to call her later. First, I had to get through the morning. I knew I would not be able to function if I tried to assimilate this information right then, and I only had about fifteen minutes before I needed to leave for the service. I decided to go sit in Mark's office and close the door to see if I could compose myself.

I sat down at his desk and let a few tears drop from my eyes. Then I felt that I needed to write. I didn't know what was going to come out, but I obeyed my instinct, picked up a pen, and pulled out a piece of scratch paper. Within a few minutes a short poem flowed without hesitation. It seemed right. I walked out the door with only the poem in my hand and went to face Mark's life.

EYES

When I arrived at The Nature Center, people were starting to gather. As we drove into the parking lot, I saw Mark's best friend Randy. I also saw my dear friend Joe getting out of his car. I thought that with both of them there, I might make it through walking in, at least.

I remembered the first time I'd met Joe. It was at a real estate seminar, where we ended up sitting next to each other. He was very serious and businesslike at first, but by the end of the day we were laughing and telling each other our latest life lessons.

It had been an instant bond that was now going to serve a different purpose; Joe was going to be strength for me.

I got out of my car, and the sadness I perceived in the gray clouds smothered me like a thick, wet blanket. Then the thought that this should be Mark's fiftieth birthday party rather than his memorial service slammed into my head and caused physical pain. I almost couldn't stand it. But then I heard, "Sweetie, it's okay, I'm here."

Mark's voice lifted my shoulders a little bit, and as I looked up I started to feel *his* strength build within me. It was as if he was flowing positive energy into my cells.

Then I heard, "This is so much better than my fiftieth birthday would have been. So many of these people would not have come to a party like that. Plus I can see and hear them *all* now. I get to listen to all of their comments, even if they are on the other side of the Center. Thank you for this day."

Mark was so near here. It felt as though he was completely surrounding me.

I went over to Joe and said, "You are one of my closest friends. I may need you at different times during this whole thing. Would you stay by me, please? You don't have to stand right next to me, but as long as I can see you or get to you easily, that would be helpful."

He said, "Of course."

We walked over to Randy, and he gave me a hug. The tears started to flow. I didn't know if I would cry the whole morning, but I did then. Randy and Mark were so close. I'm sure in many ways he would miss Mark almost as much as I would—maybe more. This was going to be so difficult; Mark was so close to so many people.

The walkway into the venue was a dirt path. It was deathly quiet because of the gray blanket of clouds covering us. It felt as if there wasn't a breath of air.

I felt nervous that there would be too many people there, and at the same time I also felt nervous that there wouldn't be *enough* people there. I was scared that when I spoke, the words would all come out wrong. I was worried that it would rain. I started to have trouble breathing.

I heard, "It's perfect," and I began to breathe.

When I got to the front of the Center, I couldn't bring myself to go into the seating area. I stood near the entrance and watched as person after person slowly paced in.

At some point I looked at my watch and noticed it was only five minutes until we were supposed to start. I looked toward the line of people still waiting to sign the guest book. My concern of too few people was not a problem anymore; the line was still at least one hundred people long, reaching out to the parking lot.

Their expressions were mixed: Some were smiling and laughing because they had run into dear friends from years past; others were somber and sad, feeling the void deeply.

I was a bit overwhelmed and numb. Person after person came up to me, greeted me warmly, hugged me, and gave me a small piece of his or her soul. It reminded me, in some ways, of our wedding. And even though this event was not expected to be uplifting, in both instances I *was* lifted up—by the guests themselves.

I looked up to the sky and realized we were not going to escape rain. I glanced around and was relieved to see there were areas around the seating that were covered, and that many people had brought umbrellas.

I also saw Joe out of the corner of my eye. He had stayed near me. I needed him *now*; I couldn't handle more people. I reached over and held his hand.

I wondered what people would think of me holding a man's hand at my husband's funeral, but the thought didn't last long. I didn't much care. It was important to me, and that was what mattered in the moment. I needed a person who understood me to be touching me. I didn't have Mark; right now I had Joe. I was going to have that, no matter what anyone thought.

Most of the people were sitting down when I saw my dad walking in my direction. I noticed I had a hard time looking at him. The memory of last Wednesday morning seemed much sharper today in my dad's presence. He'd been the one with me when I stood over Mark's body on the stretcher and realized he was really gone. I felt a stab of pain in my stomach.

He came up to me and said, "Jen, you need to get seated. The service needs to start."

I thought, "Right, it won't start without me, and I have to sit in front where everyone can see me . . . Okay. I can do this."

I looked at Joe and nodded. We walked over to the front row and sat down next to my mom.

As we were getting settled, I felt a tiny drop of rain on my cheek. Of course. *A tear. Mine? His? Both, I think.*

Sabrina, my neighbor, counselor, and friend, was standing at the front behind a podium. She took a slow, deep breath, asked the audience to do the same, and then she began. As she talked about Mark, she started to tell a story about the first item on the list of his traits, generosity. My heart started to pound. What if nobody spoke? If nobody else was willing to get up and speak about him, the service would only be about ten minutes long.

She came to the point where she asked people from the audience to give comments. I wanted so badly for Randy to tell the story of when Mark gave him his tie in the parking garage.

I looked over, but Randy wasn't getting up. I waited another moment. I was afraid she was going to move on, so I stood up. I wasn't really prepared to speak so soon, but I just couldn't let the story be lost forever.

I tried desperately to tell the story, but it came out all wrong. I looked over at Randy with pleading eyes and asked him to help on each part. Finally I just said, "Randy, are you sure you can't come up here and tell the story?"

He smiled and came to my rescue.

I was so relieved. I desperately needed people to talk about Mark. I needed people to stand up and share how he changed their lives. I needed him to be remembered for the amazing man he was. I couldn't do it all myself, and luckily I wasn't going to have to.

Over the next two hours the rain fell at times, while at others the sun broke through the clouds. Twenty-five people stood and shared stories about Mark. Our neighbors told stories about how he helped them, knew their names, and always smiled and waved. Family members spoke of the sweet boy he was and his devotion to them as he got older. His friends talked about his hunting, golf, and work stories, and my friends talked about his place in my life.

After the fifth or sixth story from Mark's buddies about hunting, fishing, golfing, skiing, and laughing, I thought to myself how lucky I was to have been with a man who was so loved by his male friends but who also cherished women.

I remembered a time when we went to The Antique Car Races in Monterey, California. We met my dad, uncle, brother, sister-in-law, and my cousin and her husband there for a long weekend.

The weather was cool and crisp, the ocean was a balmy blue-green, and the cars were perfectly restored. We spent the whole first day walking around, looking at the cars and watching races.

The next morning my sister and I wanted to go explore the aquarium and go to Carmel rather than to the car races again. We asked if anyone else wanted to join us. My dad and uncle looked at us like we were crazy; they were here to see cars and see cars they would. My uncle teasingly said, "No self-respecting man would give up cars for fish and antiques."

Mark said, "I think I'll go with the ladies."

My heart melted. I was so happy he wanted to go with us. I looked at him and he winked.

Later he told me that my dad and uncle missed the boat. He got to spend the day with two hot chicks by himself and they got to go look at some metal. What kind of fools were they?

At one point, Jill, a longtime friend of mine, stood up and told a story.

She said, "You know, Jen and I were pretty close friends. One day she came over to my house and pulled out three pieces of paper. I asked her what they were, and she said, 'These are all of the things I want in a man.'

"I looked down the list, and there was everything from what he looked like to his values and beliefs. I didn't want to be too discouraging, but I was older than her and had been married before, and this list was *long*!

"I looked at her and said, 'Good luck with that' never thinking she would actually meet someone to fit the bill.

"However, the first time I met Mark, I knew she had found him. He was strong enough to handle her, but also gentle enough to let her be herself. I knew immediately."

As Jill was speaking, I remembered our first date.

May 2000

I was a little nervous to meet this man I'd only talked to through an online dating site. He seemed nice and funny in his emails, but I had already met several other men and had not been impressed. Even so, I was still hopeful to meet someone who would be fun and a good fit.

I arrived at the restaurant a little early and was sitting on a bench outside in the sun. I looked up and noticed a car driving into the parking lot. The man at the wheel was smiling brightly and waving at me. Was this him? Wow!

I was struck by how open he was at first sight. My

heart warmed and skipped a beat. I could hardly wait for him to park and come over.

When he did, he smiled and said, "Jennifer?"

"Yes. Mark?"

He came closer and gave me a hug. I was a little taken aback, as nobody had done that at the start of a first date before. However, it felt familiar and therefore okay. Then he walked over and held the door open for me, and we went inside the restaurant.

He went around the table to pull out my chair, and we sat down. Before he even picked up the menu he said, "So, tell me about yourself."

I said, "What would you like to know?"

He said, "What is your family like?"

My first thought was, "That's interesting, no other man ever asked me about my family, and certainly not before he ordered his food."

I said, "Okay, well, I have two brothers and five sisters, and I get along really well with all of them."

"Wow, I bet your house was loud when you were kids."

"Actually it wasn't. My parents divorced when I was seven and my brother was five. My mom and dad are both remarried and have been for years. I only had my brother in the house with me when we were growing up. The rest are step-, half-, and in-laws."

I figured he would have a bunch of questions. Most people didn't understand the complexities of my family with the first explanation.

Instead, he said, "That's pretty cool. I'm kind of the same way. My parents divorced when I was five and my sister was seven. Both of my parents are remarried and have been for almost forty years. I have two sisters and two brothers but only grew up in the same house with my older sister."

I was about to say how that was interesting that we had similar families when Mark said, "Do you know what you want to eat?"

I told him I was going to get the chef's special.

The waiter came over to our table and said, "My name is James. Are you ready to order?"

Mark said, "Yes, James, the lady would like the chef's special, and I'll take the kung pao chicken."

I was a little surprised. Even though I was thirty years old and had been dating for ten years, no man had ever ordered my meal for me. Having grown up in California where things were a bit more relaxed with dating, I wasn't used to such chivalry. I was such a go-getter in business and life in general, and the gesture made me relax. I felt that I didn't have to handle everything. I felt that I was sitting across the table from a real *man*.

I smiled at Mark. I don't know if he knew why. But he said, "Your smile lights up the room."

I laughed. "Well, I'm happy."

"Tell me about where you grew up."

"That's kind of a long story. How about I give you the two-minute version?"

He smiled. "I'll take it. But some other time you can give me the long version, too."

I told him that both of my dads had been in the military and how we had moved around a lot when I was a kid; as a child I didn't like the moving, but now as an adult I realized that the moving helped me be adaptable and make friends easily.

I told him about my swimming and how I'd started when I was seven and had continued all the way through college, even swimming on a master's team for a few years after college.

"I'm probably boring you with all of this."

He said, "Absolutely not. Your life is very interesting."

"Well, tell me about yours."

"Now *that* would be boring." We both knew it wasn't true and laughed.

He told me about growing up on a farm with his mom and stepdad. He said that when he was nine he'd even owned a horse. I asked him how that came about.

"Well, my grandfather had a horse, and one year she had a colt. I wanted that colt so bad that I told my grandfather I wanted to buy her.

"He said, 'Well, son, horses know their worth. Bring your money to the barn on Saturday and we'll strike a deal.'

"I didn't know what he was talking about but I showed up right on time. I brought all of the money I had saved my whole life, which was about forty dollars."

He smiled and stopped telling the story. I looked at him. "What?"

He laughed. "My grandfather and I were very close. He was a kind and gentle man, but this day he had a little sneaky streak in him, and I'll always remember it.

"When I got to the barn, my grandfather walked over. He took my hand and said, 'Let's go see how much the little girl thinks she's worth.' I was so worried I wouldn't have enough money that I was trembling.

"As we were walking toward the barn my grandfather said, 'Horses are worth ten dollars for every time they roll over in the dirt. I wonder how much she will cost you?'

"When we arrived at the stall, my grandfather opened the door and the colt walked out to see us. She sniffed my leg and then immediately dropped down into the dust and started to roll over.

"She kept rolling and rolling. I was so sad when she got to the fifth one that I almost started to cry. Right then my grandfather started laughing. She just kept rolling and rolling. Then he kneeled down to me and said, 'If we stay here all day she won't stop. She's yours. No need to give me your money, son.'

"I was so relieved. I jumped up and clapped my hands. That night I named her Windy because I just knew she would be as fast as the wind."

I watched Mark as he told the story. It was clear how he felt about his horse—and his grandfather.

Our food came, and we talked and laughed some more. Near the end of the meal Mark and I were discussing our experience of online dating. He said, "You know, I've met quite a few people, but I've not been very impressed by many of them. I'd even go so far as to say that the majority of them should probably abstain from procreating."

I laughed out loud, knowing exactly what he meant.

And then he said, "But you, on the other hand, should definitely procreate."

I laughed again, but not quite as hard. I thought, "Did he just say I should have kids? Did he mean with him? That was kind of gutsy for a first date. I might like this guy."

During the entire two-hour memorial service you could have heard a pin drop, except for whomever was speaking. Nobody left. It seemed as if nobody even moved.

At one point the line of people talking had come to an end. I was nervous, because I had not shared the poem I had written. I also wanted to play the last message Mark had left on my phone when he was at Sam's ranch, hunting with his buddies the weekend before he died.

I let go of the grip I had on Joe's hand and stood, slowly getting my feet under me. I walked up the stairs to the podium. Sabrina was there waiting.

I was so nervous about what to do that I whispered in her ear, "I am thinking of playing the message he left me last weekend. Do you think that would be okay?"

"What do you think?"

"I want them to hear his voice once more."

She nodded at me and smiled.

I turned to face the audience and stopped. The sun had blinked out from behind the clouds for a moment. I looked around slowly for a few seconds, seeing Mark's life reflected in the audience's eyes.

Seated and standing in front of me were parents, aunts, uncles, cousins, nieces, nephews, brothers, sisters, friends, neighbors, business associates . . . you name it. There were over four hundred people I was sharing this day with.

I took a deep breath to try to stop my body from shaking; it didn't work. I moved the microphone closer and decided to start by reading the poem. I took it out of my pocket, unfolded the wrinkled paper, and looked out at the audience one more time.

I was scared I wouldn't have a voice. They were looking at me expectantly. I knew I would have to start to say something at some

point, but each moment got harder. I looked down and forced the
first word out of my mouth.

> I wanted to speak but wasn't sure if I could.
> Many told me I didn't have to, one told me I should.

> His life was that of love.
> He spread it wherever he could.

> Please know he continues that here and forever through
> me, his boys, his family, and all who he touched.

> His days with us in person seemed way too short
> But know he had a plan and would have it no other way.

> He continues forever wrapping us warmly in his arms.
> We are blessed by his love every moment of every day.

> Mark was and *is* . . . extraordinary.

When I finished I looked up through my tears to a mix of
emotions. People seemed to be waiting for more, but I didn't have
any more. There was a well of darkness inside me that was going to
stay there. Then I thought of the phone message. I had to give this
gift. I took out my phone and found the message. I put it up to the
microphone and we all heard,

Hey, sweetie, it's about 11:15, and we are just heading up the road to Sam's house to clean the three deer I got this morning. That's a good thing. [He was obviously smiling.]

I should be home around five-ish or so. I'm still on track to be on time. Anyway, I just called to say hello and I love you; I can't wait to see you and the boys. Bye.

I don't think people were prepared to hear his voice. It instantly and sharply brought his energy into the space. His voice conveyed his generosity, his love, his tenderness, and his strength more than any of my words could have.

By the end of the message most people had tears running down their faces. The sound of his voice had penetrated their hearts. He was there; I felt him. Many others told me later they did as well.

PIÑATA

After the service we had a "party" for the kids with lunch, cake, and a piñata of Mr. Incredible that the boys chose because their daddy was so incredible. At one point during lunch I looked up and realized Connor was not in my sight. I started to feel a little panic. I looked around more and realized he really wasn't there.

As I raced from one side of the Center to the other, I called his name over and over, and each time my pitch got a little higher and a little louder as the fear showed itself through my voice. Mom found him. Though it was probably only a couple of minutes from when I noticed he was gone until I heard "Jen, I found him," it felt like an eternity.

He was up on top of a castle-like structure with his Aunt Kathy. When I heard my sister say, "He's up here, Jen!" I bent over in relief and took a few deep breaths. When he came down, I hugged him and considered telling him not to do that again, but it seemed silly. I wondered, "Is this how it's going to be now that I'm on my own? Am I going to be scared whenever I can't see my children?"

After we finished lunch, my mom cut the cake and gave out giant pieces to all of the kids. The boys and I walked over to sit on a bench and enjoy the sunshine that had settled over the huge oak trees.

I finished my cake, and when I looked up I saw a friend who I hadn't seen in years. Connor got up with me to go say hi, but Brannon, who liked to savor his sweets, stayed on the bench, slowly eating his cake. I could watch him so I went and hugged my friend.

After a minute I looked back at Brannon. His eyes were closed in bliss, tasting the sweet frosting. I noticed that David, Mark's friend who had been a groomsman at our wedding, was now sitting next to him. The sun was shining brightly on both of them. I saw that David was watching Brannon intently.

David seemed to be enraptured with my son. He had a son who was in between the ages of Connor and Brannon, so I imagined he may have been thinking how lucky he was to be alive and experiencing life with his son and Brannon, unlike Mark.

The moment seemed to stretch out and slow down. It etched itself on me, filling me with sadness because Mark was not there, but at the same time delight that I was still alive and able to physically be with our children. However, I wasn't sure how I was going to be everything for these little boys.

Both of the boys' teachers had come to the party. They came over to me. I looked at Connor's teacher and said, "I don't know what to do about school."

"Don't worry. I've worked at this school for thirty years, and we have dealt with this in the past. The boys will be fine."

"When should they go back?"

"As soon as you are ready, but don't wait too long. My understanding is that having them be back on their regular schedule can be extremely comforting for them.

"What have you told the boys about your beliefs?"

I wondered why she was interested, so I asked her.

"The boys will have lots of questions. They may even be more open about it at school because they don't have the pressure of parents or family. We like to make sure our explanations either match the parent's or that we refer them to you for answers."

It felt comforting to have people who were going to be in the boys' lives who would help support me in whatever I did. No wonder I pressed so hard a year ago to get them both into that school. They had been on a waiting list for over a year, but for some reason I *knew* they should go there.

Next the kids all lined up to smash the piñata. After they were done, a subtle tightness started to twist inside me. I felt as if I couldn't go home. However, the very next thought was that I had to be strong for the boys, and that realization took over. I walked over to them, kneeled down, and said, "You guys ready to go?"

They said, "Yep!"

I took one of each of their little hands in mine and we turned to walk out.

On our way out my friend Alissa, who had helped Jeremy with the catering, ran over and said, "Jen, we have a lot of food left. Many of the people who came to the service left before the food was served. Do you know what you want to do with it?"

I had no idea. She said, "If you don't, I was thinking we might donate it to the fire department where the paramedics work—the ones who came to your home last week."

I looked at her for a second and put my hand over my mouth.

I suddenly understood why the paramedic who stood in front of my bedroom door the morning Mark died had triggered something in me: I knew him. Mark and I had taken coffee to the firemen and paramedics and toured the station several times. Mark had taken the boys there probably five times in the last year alone.

The paramedic who had come to our home on the morning Mark had died had recognized our family. He knew us. No wonder he had been so gentle. He had not wanted to block the door. He'd not wanted to be there—or maybe he had.

I nodded my head. "Take them the food. That's perfect. Thank you."

I couldn't say anything else, so I started walking out with the boys.

We were almost to the exit when a friend pulled us away from the group we were walking in. He and his wife had been standing there waiting. He said, "Jennifer, I just wanted to thank you."

I didn't know what he was talking about, so I let him go on. He said, "You have changed our lives. This service has shown us how to live differently. We have already started making changes, including this."

He lifted up their arms and showed me they were holding hands.

I nodded my head, closed my eyes, and smiled. This was what I wanted: for Mark's life to make a difference.

Then he said, "Another thing. I don't think you know this, but my wife is a widow. I am her second husband."

I was shocked. I had always thought they had been married forever.

He said, "I had to be extra fantastic to her because her first husband was so amazing."

I smiled because I knew he was hinting around that I might get married again someday. I also knew that at a later date I might actually want to think about that, but not right now.

Then his wife said, "If you ever want to talk to me about what you are going through, please call. I had small children as well."

With those words I felt that I could go home. I knew life would be hard but that it would sort itself out at some point, and that whatever support I needed would show up when I needed it. I thanked them, tightened my grasp a little on Connor and Brannon's hands, and we walked out together.

THE ZOO

The day after the memorial I decided to start the boys back in school. They had been out for a week, and I didn't want them to wait any longer before getting back into their routine.

My mom asked if I wanted her to take them, but I said no.

As I pulled into the school driveway where I dropped them off, I realized it might not have been a good idea for me to take them. I knew *they* would be okay in school, but I wasn't sure *I* could handle watching them walk away from me.

We got up to the front of the line, and I was getting a bit more nervous. The boys unbuckled their seatbelts, grabbed their lunch boxes, and hugged me. I almost started to cry. As they hopped out I said, "I love you! See you after school."

I tried my best not to have my voice sound as strained as it felt. How could I be gone from them for six hours? They ran off as if nothing were different.

I pulled forward to get out of the way of the next car, and the pain exploded in me. Mark had been the person who dropped them off almost every morning. He should have been here. This felt so wrong!

After a few minutes I knew the tears would not stop for a long time, so I started the car anyway and pulled out of the parking lot.

When I drove into the garage at home, I turned off the car and tried to wipe off my face so people wouldn't know how upset I was. I couldn't find any tissues. I grabbed my purse and walked in the door, trying to avoid anyone's eyes as I went upstairs to my room as fast as I could.

I heard my mom talking to my brother in the kitchen. I heard his wife and my nephews playing in the living room. The normalcy of it was unbearable. I shut myself in my room and got in the shower, letting the hot water run over my body until I couldn't feel my back anymore.

When I didn't think I could cry any more I got out, got dressed, and went downstairs to face people.

My brother and his family were flying home that day, but their flight wasn't leaving for several hours. My two sisters had offered to help me with anything I needed while my brother took his boys to the zoo.

I had asked them if they would help me remove Mark's personal things from his office so Julie could work in there more easily.

Mark was a very organized person on the outside, but the inside of his desk drawers was a totally different story. He had personal items mixed in with all of his work, so much that even I could hardly tell it apart. I knew there was no way I was going to be able to mentally or emotionally handle separating out those things anytime soon.

So as my sisters sat on the floor dividing photos, files, books, trinkets, and receipts into boxes, I played with my nephews and decided I wanted to go to the zoo with them.

Before I left, I peeked in the office and said, "Do you need anything from me before we leave?"

Jennifer, my sister-in-law, pointed out the window and said, "I think we have the office handled, but how much did the house across the street sell for?"

"About three hundred thousand dollars."

Her eyes widened in surprise. I knew that was quite a bit less than she had paid for her much smaller home in California. I told her that three hundred thousand was about the average price in our neighborhood.

Then she said, "Man! We would love to move out here, but there is no way because Jeremy would have to have a job."

I looked at her, sitting there on the floor of Mark's office going through his things, and suddenly a flash of light hit me; for an instant I was literally blinded. Then it seemed as if everything went into slow motion.

I could hear my own voice trembling when I said, "Well, there might be an opening in sales."

She had a piece of paper in her hand, and it stopped in mid-air when she lifted her eyes to mine. Then I watched like a spectator as she stood up, came over, and wrapped her arms around me.

When I felt her touch, it triggered my ability to feel, and we both started crying. She said in my ear, "We would do anything for you. I would move here. It's between you and Jeremy."

I couldn't believe what she was saying. As far as I knew they had never considered moving. Their boys were almost the same age as Connor and Brannon. What an incredible opportunity for our families to be closer and for a very large open space in our lives to be partly filled. I didn't want to let go of her.

Eventually she let go, and I told her I would talk to Jeremy and see what he thought. As we were driving to the zoo I kicked the idea around in my head. The more I thought about it, the more it made sense. My brother had a technical background just like Mark and had worked in sales and marketing successfully for over seven years. He had never worked in the same industry, but I knew once he learned the business he'd be a very good fit.

However, the most important factor in my mind was that

I trusted him with my life and my children's lives. He loved us; therefore I knew he would take care of the business as if it were his. Nobody else in the world would do that—nobody; it didn't matter how experienced they were. Well, maybe Randy would, but he had told me he was not interested. When he'd said that, I didn't want to believe him. Now I thought maybe I knew why it was working out this way.

We pulled into a parking spot at the zoo, and I was thinking about how I would bring up the subject with Jeremy. I wasn't sure what to say, but I knew one thing: My brother had always been able to handle my directness. So as we were walking in I looked over at him and said, "Would you consider taking over Mark's job?"

He stopped in his tracks as if he had hit a brick wall. He raised his eyebrows, took in a big breath, and said, "Now *that* is an interesting question."

My heart smiled. At least he didn't just say no. I took it as an optimistic "maybe."

I thought he was done talking, but then he said, "Now that I think of it, Mark called me about two or three months ago out of the blue. When I picked up the phone he said, 'Hey there, brother-man,' like he always did. Then after our conversation was over, he jokingly said, 'Why don't you move out here and go to work with me?'"

Jeremy was smiling. "I thought he was kidding."

My heart was so full. To have my brother here would be the most incredible blessing I could imagine. We had been extremely close our whole lives but hadn't lived near each other in over fifteen years. To have him and his family live near us would be nothing less than a godsend.

Jeremy said he would talk it over with Jen, that we could talk about some details this week, and that they would make a decision soon, one way or the other. He knew I had to hire someone to take care of the customers in a timely manner, and he didn't want to hold me up if they decided they couldn't move.

Later that day they flew home. The house seemed very empty. I was walking into the kitchen when the phone rang.

It was a friend of Mark's named Paul. I'd met him briefly a couple of times but didn't know him very well. He had known Mark for many years and had worked in the same business. He asked me if there was anything he could do to help out, because he wasn't employed at the moment and had a lot of time on his hands.

I said, "Maybe you can help me and Julie get through the next week or two and then maybe you can help train Jeremy if he comes to work for us."

He agreed wholeheartedly, and we ironed out some details on what I would pay him and when he would start.

Then he said, "Hey, Jen, I'm down the street from where your partner's office is right now. I know them pretty well. I'll go have lunch with them and tell them I'm helping you."

"That's fine with me, but I'd like to be the one to talk to them about hiring my brother. Please don't mention it."

"Sure. No problem. I'll see you in a couple of days and we can get started."

ONE WEEK

I woke up Wednesday morning and a thought ran into my head: Mark's body.

My dad and Jeremy had done such a good job of taking care of everything that I didn't even know what was going on with Mark. I picked up the phone and called Jeremy.

He answered on the first ring and said, "Is everything okay?"

"Yes, I wanted to make sure you got home okay."

"Yeah, no problems . . . Was there something else?"

I wasn't sure what words to use. I knew what I wanted to ask, but the syllables wouldn't form in my mouth.

"Mark."

"Oh . . . Yes. We didn't talk with you about it much."

I couldn't say anything else.

"Do you want me to just tell you?" he said.

"Uh-huh."

"Um, well, we had to wait a couple of days after the autopsy because there was not a time available for the cremation. Dad had said he would be the witness."

I thought, "God! Someone had to witness it?"

"When he went, he took his brother with him, and it's a good thing he did. At the last minute Dad couldn't do it. "

I was weeping. Dad and Mark were friends; he loved Mark like a son. He laughed out loud with him like one of the guys. He cherished Mark; he had a bond with him . . . He couldn't do it. I'm sure that shocked him, but it didn't surprise me.

Jeremy said, "Are you okay?"

"Yes." My voice cracked. "Go on."

"We don't have to do this right now," he said.

"I know. But it's been a week. I need to know."

"Okay. Well, Dad's going to pick up the ashes and the urn tomorrow and keep them until you're ready to decide what you want to do with them."

I was so relieved. I didn't think I could handle seeing the box. Then guilt swept over me. Shouldn't I want him close? What was wrong with me? I just didn't feel like it was him anymore. "He" was communicating with me. "He" didn't have a body anymore. His body was like all of the stuff in our house: useless, really.

I thanked Jeremy and hung up.

Two days later Jeremy called. When I picked up the phone and said hello I was thrilled to hear his voice on the line. I knew he and Jen had been talking about whether or not they would move and help me with the business, and I was excited and nervous to hear what they had been discussing.

Jeremy instinctively knew I'd been waiting to know what their decision was, so he started right in.

"We've pretty much decided to move."

My heart jumped!

"Is there something specific that's keeping you from making the final decision?"

"Yes. We just need to know if you know a real estate agent who can help us find a house."

We both started laughing.

I said, "Is that it?"

"Yes. We're moving. I'll be there in just over two weeks. I have to give my boss notice."

I could hardly believe what I was hearing. My brother and his family were going to move and live by us? It felt unreal, and at the same time it felt right.

"I'm so happy. I know you guys are going to love it here. I know this is a huge decision. Thank you so much."

"No problem. We want to. Thanks for trusting me and for giving us the opportunity."

When he said those words I knew that the move and Jeremy working for the company *were* right. If he was looking at this as an opportunity rather than an obligation, then he was thinking straight and not just making a knee-jerk reaction to an emergency situation. This was going to be the opportunity of a lifetime for him.

However, I also knew he was my brother and was stepping up to a big load on his shoulders. If he was here, I was sure there would be times when I'd lean on him as I would nobody else. I was closer to him than anyone, regardless of the years we had spent apart.

I told him I'd help him with a house and moving and we hung up. Then I walked into the living room and told the boys that their cousins were moving to town! They started running around the house and yelling with their arms in the air.

Such joy. So soon.

VALENTINE'S DAY

A few days later the dust had settled a bit. Other than my mom and stepdad, everyone had left, so I had to face Valentine's Day, the day Mark had asked me to marry him, more alone than I had wanted to be.

As Valentine's Day approached, my mother and I developed a nightly ritual. After I finished getting ready for bed, I walked downstairs and into the living room, where Mom was sitting on the couch reading. I turned off all of the lights except for the one behind us in the kitchen, sat down next to her, and gently laid my head in her lap.

She put her hand on my forehead and started to stroke my hair and face. I looked at the family picture on the wall of Mark, me, and the boys, and I cried. She never said anything until I did.

Typically it went something like this:

"I can't believe this is my life."

Mom would mumble, "Mmm-hmm."

"I'm not sure what I should do or even if I *can* do this by myself. At least when people get divorced the other person is still there as a backup. I just can't *believe* this is my life."

Some nights were worse than others. Sometimes I would just lie there and let her stroke my head until the pain seemed to go away a little. Other times I wouldn't be able to stop crying, and she'd start, too.

The time on the couch with my mother became sacred. It seemed that it was the only time I had each day where I could *feel* without distraction. She was my refuge.

Every day, from the moment I woke up until the moment I lay down with my mom, it was go, go, go. With the kids, Mark's work, my work, and even people just calling to make sure I was okay, I was overwhelmed and operating completely on autopilot. There was no real time to grieve, as each day blended into the next . . . that is, until Valentine's Day, the anniversary of the day Mark had asked me to marry him.

That morning, after my shower, I looked at our wedding rings, sitting on the counter together. It was so hard to believe he had given me my ring just eight years ago and that he was already gone. When he'd bought it he had meant for it to be on my finger my whole life. I could feel the sadness getting larger and larger in my body. I was terrified of where my thoughts would go with this topic.

Then I heard him say, "Don't wear the rings and torture yourself today. There is no need. They're just rings. The real heart of what we had we still have."

I didn't really want to hear what he was saying, though; it was too soon. He was still *gone*. Who was he to try to take away *my* pain? I deserved to feel it. I pushed him out of my mind and away from me and decided to wear my ring.

Later in the day I had the urge to hear his voice. I wanted to experience the physical resonance, however—the sound, not just a thought. It was different.

While I was eating lunch I remembered the voice mail message Mark had left on my phone the weekend before he died. It had been two weeks since he left the message. I went to get my phone. I *was* going to get to hear his voice! I was so excited.

I hit the button for voice mail and went through the menu to get to the saved messages, and then I heard, "There are no saved messages at this time."

I couldn't believe it. *No!* My stomach twisted and turned. I put my head down into my hands and gripped the sides of my hair. How could I have been so stupid as to not record it onto something else before it was automatically erased?

Then I suddenly remembered I had asked my cousin to videotape the memorial service, and that I had decided to play the message there. I still had it. The anxiety started to flow out of me. I might not have been able to listen to him right then, but I would hear his voice say "I love you" again.

During the day I found myself repeatedly telling people that Mark had asked me to marry him eight years ago. I told everyone I saw; it was as though I had to vent a little of the pain out into the world on whomever came across my path that day. I couldn't hold it all in.

Mark and I had made plans to go to a winery for dinner with three other couples. I had debated cancelling but wondered if maybe I should go. I thought that *not* going might be worse. But I didn't think it through. I asked my stepdad if he would go with me.

"Of course, if you want me to."

As I was getting ready, I noticed how different it felt to be putting on clothes and makeup when it wasn't for my husband. It felt less important, as if it wouldn't be appreciated, at least not in the way Mark would have appreciated the effort. I went through the motions anyway, just because . . . what else was I going to do?

We drove to the winery with another couple. When we got there, my stepdad got out first and held the door to the car for the rest of us. Mark would have done that.

Then we started to walk in. Mark would have taken my hand. The absence of having my hand held was so loud in my thoughts.

I walked a few steps, but I couldn't help it; I reached out and took my stepdad's arm. That was okay. At least I was touching a warm human being who cared about me.

All during the meal everything felt forced. I was beginning to feel that I shouldn't be there. I wondered if anyone was having any fun at all or if they were all thinking, "It's just so sad." I almost couldn't stay in my chair.

I noticed that I either wasn't talking much when others were talking, or I was talking too much when they weren't. I felt as if I was trying to compensate for what people weren't saying. I felt I was trying to fill up the silent moments so that nobody could really think about how horrible it was that Mark wasn't there. It was going to be a long night. I began to regret my decision to come.

Finally everyone was done and it was time to go. I was exhausted. When we got home, I decided to immediately go to bed to escape the pain. I walked upstairs and into my closet, and when I looked at Mark's clothes, a wave of sadness hit me so hard I broke down and crumbled to the floor, sobbing.

I couldn't stop the barrage of pain and sadness from rolling through me. I don't know how long I lay there curled up in a ball, but at some point I heard Mark say, "Everything is going to be okay."

His voice was like a healing salve on a wound. It didn't take the wound away, but it kept the air from making the pain worse.

With that little extra boost, the tears started to subside. I didn't move from the floor, but I started to take some deep breaths and then I heard, "You need to *do* something."

"I know, I shouldn't just lie here on the floor. If I get up and move around, it won't feel as bad."

I sat up and started to think of something to do. I wondered if I should go check emails. The only problem was that when I did, I would usually end up crying more than ever because of the condolence messages.

Instead I decided to go down into Mark's office and go through the personal files I'd been avoiding, those that my sisters had organized the week before. I had been concerned that there might be something I needed to take care of, but up until this point I'd been staying away from his office.

I pulled myself up off the floor and went downstairs. When I walked into his office, I sat down at his desk, took a deep breath, and opened the drawer. I flipped through some of the files, just looking at the names on the top. There didn't seem to be anything important that needed immediate attention.

Then I saw he had a health insurance file. I knew I had an identical file in my desk upstairs. I didn't understand why he had this file. I felt compelled to open it. I pulled it out, set it on my lap, and carefully lifted the cover. Lying on top of all the papers was a page that didn't fit in. It was smaller than all of the other documents. I looked a little closer.

It seemed to be a paid receipt for a *life* insurance policy.

As I read the first few lines, I realized it was a policy that I thought he had allowed to lapse. But for some reason this invoice showed he had paid the yearly premium just three months ago.

I was stunned. I put my hand up to my forehead and put my elbow on the desk. I thought, "If it's true and I do get this money, it would help me pay for Jeremy to take over your work. I wouldn't have to worry about that part of it. You just gave me my *brother*."

At that moment I heard, "Happy Valentine's Day."

PAUL

On Monday morning Mark's friend Paul showed up at the house to help me with the business. When he walked in, I asked him to sit down at the table for a few minutes so we could get on the same page. I wanted to tell him about Jeremy so we could work out a plan to get him trained.

I said, "Jeremy has decided to take the job and move here."

Paul didn't say anything.

"I'd like to put a plan together to train him. How long do you think you can work with us?"

"Okay. Well, what I need to do right now is really get into the details of the business and make sure there aren't any fires that need to be put out. Then we can make a plan to train Jeremy."

"That sounds good."

I showed him where the files were and then told him I was going to go upstairs while he worked. The first thing I wanted to do was call our financial partners to talk to them about Jeremy.

As I was turning to leave, Paul put his hand on my arm, stopped me, and said, "Oh, by the way, Jen, I just need to let you know, I ended up telling your financial partners that you were thinking of hiring your brother."

I stood there for a second trying to grasp what he had said.

I thought there was no way he was serious. I had made it clear I didn't want him to say anything to them. I was so upset I didn't know what to say.

"What happened?" I asked, finally.

"Well, during lunch they asked if I was going to work here full time, and it just slipped out that you were considering hiring Jeremy."

The fire of anger burned through my veins. I couldn't believe what he was saying. Why would he tell them? I turned and went upstairs to think.

When I sat down at my desk my mind was reeling. I thought, "Maybe he didn't understand the significance of the information coming from me. Maybe he didn't hear me." I thought of every excuse to give him the benefit of the doubt.

Paul spent most of the morning working with Julie downstairs at the large dining room table. She was getting him somewhat up to speed on the different files he would need to sort out before Jeremy started.

At lunch time I went downstairs to get an update on how they were doing. Julie pulled me aside and said, "Paul knows his stuff and I'm sure he can help us get through the next week or two, but he seems very preoccupied with the messages he keeps getting from his girlfriend—so much so that I had to leave the room and go into Mark's office to get *my* work done."

I didn't know what to do. I knew Paul had been Mark's friend for almost twenty years and he said that he would do anything to help us, but I was starting to get a funny feeling about his "help."

I decided not to make a snap judgment. I didn't know for sure if Julie could handle the business by herself. I wasn't completely sure of anything.

After lunch Paul and I sat down and talked a little bit more about how much I was going to pay him. During this conversation he said, "Jennifer, you're making a huge mistake by hiring your brother. It's going to take him a long time to get up to speed in this industry and it will really hurt the company."

I knew he had a point about the time needed for Jeremy to get up to speed, but deep down it just felt as if Paul was trying to undermine him. I knew my brother and knew what he was capable of achieving, and I didn't have *any* reservations about hiring him. *I* was willing to take the risk, and that was what mattered.

By the end of three days it was obvious that Paul wanted me to hire him full time rather than my brother. I told him again and again that I wasn't going to do that. I felt that I had to hold him off like a hound on a rabbit, and I didn't have the strength to keep it up.

At one point my frustration was obviously showing, and my mom said, "Jen, you need to get him out of here. He is not helping."

So I finally told Paul he might as well go home. I said Julie and I would handle the business until my brother arrived. I wasn't sure how I was going to get Jeremy trained; all I knew was that I needed Paul to leave.

As he was getting ready to go, I wanted to make sure to handle any balance I owed him. I asked him to count up the number of hours he worked, and then I wrote him a check for the full, agreed-upon amount we had discussed three days before. I asked him to email me a formal invoice for my tax records when he got home. I was extremely relieved when he left.

I didn't hear from him for a couple of days. When I didn't receive an invoice, I called him and left a message reiterating that I needed to have it for my tax records. I didn't hear a word. Then finally after a week he called.

I picked up the phone in Mark's office. Jeremy had arrived that day and was sitting at the desk with me. When I saw it was Paul, I put the phone on speaker. I wanted Jeremy to hear first-hand what was happening so he could help me decide how to handle the situation.

Paul said, "What's going on? Are we going to work this out or what?"

I was a little surprised at his question. In my mind there was nothing to work out, so I said, "What do you mean?"

"I can't work with you full time from out of state. I need to move there."

I was confused. I was absolutely sure I had made it clear when he left that it wasn't going to work. "Paul, I am *not* going to hire you."

There was complete silence on the line. I looked over at Jeremy, who was dumbfounded. I waited for Paul, wondering what he was going to say. The next words I heard shook me to the bone.

"Mark would be ashamed of the decisions you are making."

I heard a roar in my head at the same time my own thoughts screamed. It was Mark, and he was furious! Mark said, "I don't think so! Get rid of him now and forever, whatever you have to do."

I couldn't believe what I was hearing, both from Paul and from Mark. The blood was pounding in my ears, and I had a sick feeling in my stomach.

I said, "Paul, don't you *ever* mention Mark's name to me again. You don't have the right anymore. There is no way I am hiring you, ever."

All I heard was a dial tone.

Jeremy said, "You obviously made the right decision."

After I hung up I was quite upset. I felt that I needed to talk to someone who knew Paul, to know who I was dealing with. I didn't know him very well and he was scaring me. His reactions seemed very strong, and I was worried he might do something to hurt the business.

I picked up the phone and called David. I knew him pretty well from my real estate team, and I thought he knew Paul from when he worked with Mark and Randy.

"Hey, Jen! What's up?"

Just the sound of a friend's voice made me feel a little better. I didn't have any energy to engage in small talk, so I just said, "I'm having some trouble with Paul."

David actually chuckled and said, "Tell me."

I told him everything that had happened.

"Jen, I've known Paul for a long time, and I'll tell you this. If he could work in a vacuum by himself, he'd be a multi-billionaire. He's brilliant, but his people skills leave a little to be desired."

I was beginning to feel better. When I told him what Paul said about Mark, he became quiet for a few moments and then said, "I'm so sorry. That's not true. Mark trusted you with everything in his life and would *completely* trust you with this decision."

Deep down I knew it was true, but hearing it from someone who knew us both helped to make it more real. It also gave me strength to handle the situation.

Within a couple of weeks I received the paid receipt, and Jeremy was ready to take on the huge task of Mark's work.

ON OUR OWN

It was unthinkable to me that my mom would ever leave, but after five weeks, I understood that she needed to go back to her own life. My step dad had gone home two weeks ago, and she needed to join him.

I dreaded her leaving. I didn't know what it would be like to be by myself with the boys in the house. I wasn't sure I was ready to find out.

When I drove her to the airport, I gave her a hug, but I didn't want to let go. She'd become more than a mom; she was my friend, confidante, companion, and my champion. She'd seen me go through the hardest emotional time in my life. I almost couldn't stand saying goodbye to her or watching her say goodbye to the boys.

That night I made dinner and the three of us sat down at the table to eat. The moment I sat down it felt different. Before this night we had always had at least a fourth person eating with us. This was the first time it was only the three of us since Mark had gone.

I felt Mark's void so deeply. I tried not to think the words, "meal time was family time," but I wasn't fast enough to stop the thought. I put my hands up over my eyes and started to cry.

Connor looked at me and gently said, "Mommy, why are you crying?"

I looked up through the tears and sat there for a minute, wondering how he didn't know, and thinking about how innocent and how open he was to be willing to ask that question.

His openness inspired me, and I said, "Because I miss Daddy."

Without missing a beat, Brannon chimed in, "Knock Knock."

Through the tears I said, "Who's there?"

"Boo!"

Knowing this was the only knock-knock joke Brannon knew, I was now anticipating the punch line to the joke. I actually smiled and said, "Boo who?"

He smiled and said, "Mommy, why are you crying?"

Instantly I started to laugh. My three-year-old was telling me the only joke he knew in order to cheer me up. And it was appropriate.

I realized I was all they had. If I was down, they would feel it would be their job to pick me up. If they were down, it was going to be my job to pick them up. It seemed unfair that at such a young age they were taking on this responsibility.

I would be as strong as possible to prevent them from having to take that position very often, but I knew that for me to be 100 percent strong and not cry in front of them was an impossibility, and probably not entirely healthy for me or for them.

We would wade through it together. We *would* make it.

On Monday morning I took the boys to school and then decided to go for a swim. I felt drained from watching them by myself most of the weekend. I knew there was a good chance I'd see people at the pool that I knew. I wasn't sure how it would go. I did know I needed to clear my head and energize my body, and swimming had never failed me in those respects.

When I walked up to the pool I saw a few people I knew, but they were all swimming. I put on my cap and jumped in the water.

After I warmed up I started to do a few sets and felt my body loosen up, my breathing become longer, and my mind drop into a rhythmic, meditative state. The blood began to flow stronger, my brain cleared, and I started to kick harder. As I did, the grime burned out of my body and I began to feel like myself.

I came to a stop to catch my breath and saw four of my friends in the lanes next to me. One of them said, "Hey. We are going to go to the coffee shop after we are done. Do you want to come with us?"

I had not taken much time in the last year or two for relaxing with friends. Mark had been the one to go to the coffee shop. Maybe it was time for me to do that.

I said, "Absolutely!"

I finished my workout and noticed that they were already gone. When I got to the coffee shop I opened the door and saw everyone sitting at a table together. I got some tea and went over to sit down.

One of the men, a guy named Rick, said, "You know, Jennifer, we used to always see Mark here with the boys."

"Yeah, Mark used to get up with the boys and go get his coffee so I could sleep in."

Then he said, "Well, it's nice to have you here. We miss him. He was a bright spot in our day—so open and warmhearted. He was very unique."

"Yes."

We sat around and talked for almost an hour. Then I said I needed to go. It felt a little too indulgent to spend so much time not being productive.

On the way home I thought, "Was that really *not* productive? It felt amazing to sit and connect with people. I think more of that will be in my future." And I smiled.

HIS PRESENCE

A week or so later I was lying in bed sobbing, curled up in a ball. The pain of missing someone I loved so much yet knew I would *never* see again was excruciating. My head throbbed, my eyes were raw, my gut was in knots. After a few minutes of crying I started to say, "I miss you so much. I ache to be close to you and touch you."

I heard, "I am closer to you now than I ever was."

My first response was to be a little put off. The words felt like a mean joke. He wasn't closer; he was gone!

Then I heard, "There aren't any boundaries between us anymore. You can finally know me as you always wanted to, and I have complete understanding and acceptance for you. Our relationship is more perfect than it ever was. I will be with you and the boys forever. I don't have to be in a body to do that."

Was he really with us? Was he closer than he used to be? Was this our new relationship? Would it really go on? I knew we had issues in our marriage, like most. But it had been a very good marriage and I missed him being there with me. This didn't seem anywhere near the same and in no way *better* than what we had before.

I thought maybe he would say something else, but as I lay there and became a little more present, it really felt as if he was waiting for me. I wondered more about his words. As I did, I realized that all of the issues between us that I had just thought of *were* gone. But weren't they gone only because *he* was gone? Of *course* we didn't fight about those things anymore. Still nothing . . .

I relaxed my body, took some deep breaths, and settled into the moment as much as I could. I thought about the times I'd heard Mark in the last weeks. Whenever I'd heard him I'd also felt warm and comforted. The communication felt easy.

I heard, "Yes, keep going with that."

I thought, "Maybe our spirits seem closer."

I heard, "YES!"

So I thought, "Okay, it is very different, yet extremely satisfying in *some* ways."

As soon as I had the thought of it being satisfying, though, my first reaction was to scream at him, "Why couldn't it be like this when you were *here?*" But as soon as I thought it, I knew that life for us was not like that.

He said, "Yes, exactly. And it's okay."

I started to think that maybe communication wasn't that way for *most* people here on earth, but maybe if it was, life might seem more peaceful. I certainly felt peaceful when we communicated now. I tried to imagine him there with me, sitting on the bed.

He said, "Thank you for believing and being willing and open enough to hear me and feel me and know the *real* me. I'm in heaven—heaven on earth within you and around you. Everything you touch I still *touch*; everything you see and feel I still *see* and *feel* because you believe. Thank you."

I thought, "There is no way you can see and feel things just because I do." I also thought, "Can't you see everything and feel *nothing* since you are not physically here?"

I did not get an answer to my question. I wondered if he was upset because I didn't believe him. However, if I was going to learn anything from this exchange it was that it was *not possible* for him to be upset with me. I stewed on everything he had said and finally drifted off to sleep sometime later.

The next night I was putting Brannon in bed. I had been struggling all day with what Mark had said the night before about being able to see, feel, and hear what I did. I decided to test his theory. I thought if I touched the boys and thought about Mark, that maybe I could tell if he was feeling what I was feeling.

As I was telling Brannon a bedtime story about dinosaurs, I leaned over and put my forehead on his. Then I intentionally thought about Mark. Suddenly I felt a spark of energy. In my mind I saw Mark's spirit jumping for joy. I saw him doing summersaults and cartwheels and yelling and laughing. While I was sitting there in shock, Brannon actually looked at me and giggled.

As a knee-jerk reaction I said, "Did you feel that?"

Brannon nodded his head. I was stunned. I didn't think he would actually say "yes." I didn't know what to do. I decided to try to be present and notice what was happening. They both sure seemed happy. Maybe Mark *could* feel what I felt.

I heard, "No, only when you put your attention on me and *want* me to feel."

He was there; it was as if he were standing in the room next to me but maybe even more powerful than a physical presence. The sensation was almost smothering, it was so strong.

After I finished saying goodnight to Brannon, I went into Connor's room. But I didn't feel like putting my forehead on him. Instead I gently laid my hand on his leg and thought of Mark as I was saying goodnight.

Mark's response to Connor was *very* different. This time there was no excitement or joy, but instead there was a deep sense of calm and strength. It was much more soothing and relaxing, not so excited and jovial. It seemed as though we were surrounded by a warm cloud.

I thought it was strange that the two experiences were so different. Maybe Mark knew the boys needed something different that night. Or maybe it was just because he had been different with the boys during his life.

Connor didn't do anything out of the ordinary, so I didn't say a word about it but just finished talking with him and got up to go.

When I was at the door I said, "Good night, I love you, and see you in the morning."

After he replied, I closed the door and started to walk away.

I took two steps and stopped.

I couldn't believe it! I realized that for the first night since Mark's passing, Connor did *not* say to me, "Mommy, I'm scared" when I left his room.

I felt a deep pressure building up in my chest; I put my hands there and closed my eyes in wonder. Connor *had* felt Mark's presence and had been soothed by it.

UNCLE JEREMY

A few days later I was sitting at my desk thinking about Jeremy and how to get him trained. Paul was obviously not an option anymore. Julie was teaching Jeremy part of what he would need to know, but there were some more technical aspects she would not be able to completely explain, as she had never done them.

I thought about whom I should contact. I decided to send out a couple of emails to people to ask for their help. I sent one to Randy and one to David. Randy, David, and Mark had worked together for seven years. Maybe one of them could point me in the right direction.

Randy responded and said Jeremy could attend some courses, which sounded promising, but unfortunately after doing some research I learned that none of the courses were being given anytime soon. This was a concern because I knew Jeremy was ready to get right into the thick of it, and I needed him to do just that.

David responded as well. I opened his email and it said, "Sure, I'd be interested in helping Jeremy get up to speed. I used to work in the same industry with the same type of customers your company serves now. In addition, I was a corporate trainer on the topic for three years. I can teach him the basics and more. It's easy. Let me know when and where."

That was interesting. I didn't know David had been a trainer. I was also a little surprised he was so willing to jump in and help so much since he was now a full time real estate agent. I wrote him back and asked if he would be willing to do a class as soon as possible. He said he could, in a couple of days.

That afternoon when the boys got home from school, I noticed they each stopped at the door to Mark's office and looked in. Jeremy was not yet working in Mark's office full time so it was empty.

When Mark had been there, the boys used to go into his office and tell him about their day and just be with him for a few minutes before they went in with the nanny. Mark would tickle them, and I would hear their laughter all the way upstairs.

It was heartbreaking to watch them look in the door and see nothing. They stood there for a few moments and then walked past and into the living room. I could only imagine how difficult it was for them to not have that as part of their day anymore.

Sabrina had told me that children process grief differently than adults. She said they don't lose the future expectations as adults do; they live in the present, so they really only feel the loss of what is right now.

When she told me that it seemed like a good thing, but at this moment it seemed horrible. It made me think that each time they looked in the office and Mark wasn't there, that they would really feel their loss. I wondered how they would respond when Jeremy was sitting there rather than Mark.

A few days later Jeremy and I went to David's house and spent the whole day getting taught the history of the industry and the more technical aspects that Julie couldn't help Jeremy learn. When we left, our heads were swimming with data, but I felt satisfied that Jeremy would be able to catch on.

It was exciting to watch Jeremy learn. It was also a relief to see how motivated David was to help us keep the business together. I didn't feel so alone anymore with the daunting task of getting Jeremy trained and keeping the business running.

As we were leaving his house, David told me that if there was anything I ever needed, to make sure to call and ask him. He said he was even willing to watch the boys for me if I ever wanted some time for myself.

I told him I'd definitely take him up on that offer.

The next day Jeremy worked all day with Julie and me, getting more into the details of our customer's accounts. When the boys got home they went straight to the office, and upon seeing Jeremy there, they acted a little shy.

Jeremy looked over at the glass door and saw them. He gave them a big grin, opened the door, and put his arms out to hug them.

They both excitedly said, "Uncle Jeremy!" and ran in.

I put my head down so they wouldn't see the tears of joy streaming down my face.

ANGER

A few weeks later it seemed that Connor was acting angry at Brannon. He was short with his brother, quick to pick fights, and was even hitting him, which was unheard-of before now.

I decided to talk to Mark about it.

That night I was lying in bed and I said, "Are you there?"

Instantly I heard, "I always am if you want me to be."

I was starting to believe him.

"Okay then, have you noticed that Connor doesn't seem happy?"

"Yes."

"Well, is there anything I can do about it? Do you know why he's so angry?"

To my surprise Mark said, "Connor is angry because somewhere deep down in his subconscious he has figured out the reason I left. The only problem is that at this moment he is incapable of seeing the whole picture. He only understands that I saved Brannon's life by leaving, not the other reasons. He feels like he lost his dad and it's his brother's fault. He's mad."

After I got over how strange the conversation was, I asked, "What do you mean by other reasons?"

"I did this for all of you, not just Brannon. Somewhere, somehow, he needs to understand the big picture."

"Is there anything I can do to help him?"

"Actually, yes. It may seem strange, but just try this. Go in his room when he is asleep and talk to him. He hears everything. His subconscious will pick up on what you say and it will help him."

At that point I wasn't sure what I should say. I was thinking that the big picture was that if Mark had stayed and Brannon had died, then Connor's life would have been much less than what he was capable of experiencing. I thought that maybe I should say Mark did this not only for Brannon, but for Connor, too.

I heard, "Yes. The truth is, had I stayed and Brannon had died, Brannon would have been *fine*. He would have been here, and here is better than fine. It's really Connor, you, and I who would have been destroyed.

"So even though I gave Brannon his life, I really gave Connor the amazing life he deserves to have with his brother and you. In addition, now his memories of me are of joy and love rather than blame, anger, and grief.

"Finally, as I have said, I was going to die eventually anyway. The timing just allowed me to give you all a gift. I really did leave for all of us, not just for Brannon. Connor needs to know and really understand this deeply, as do *you*."

I noticed myself drifting to this idea of Mark leaving for all of us. I thought about how he had always had a very tight bond with Connor and how early that bond had started. He adored Connor even before he was born.

March 2003
Mark and I were thrilled to be expecting our first child.

We were waiting for the doctor to come in for our sonogram appointment. Mark was so excited to see a picture of our baby. I'd felt little flutters of kicking, but it was nothing Mark was able to feel yet. All he had been able to experience during the pregnancy was my bad moods, weird food cravings, and me jokingly blaming him for "doing this to me!" Needless to say, he was excited to have a more tangible connection to our unborn child. He was so nervous and elated he was practically bouncing in his chair.

When the doctor came in, he explained that the machine he was using was the very latest in modern technology. He put some gel on my stomach, and as soon as he touched me with the cold metal handpiece we heard a very fast, loud, thumping noise. I was surprised by it.

The doctor said, "That's the baby's heartbeat."

As we listened, I felt as if we were being pulled together. There were three of us now; this wasn't just about Mark and me anymore.

The doctor continued with the sonogram and spent a little time showing us the arm bones, the leg bones, and the other parts of the body, and then he said, "Do you want to know if it's a boy or girl?"

Mark and I looked at each other, smiled, and nodded our heads.

"Well, you are definitely having a boy."

Mark could hardly contain himself. He had four nieces and no nephews; his dad was going to jump for joy.

Then the doctor said very seriously, "I need to talk to you about something."

The smiles left our faces as quickly as they had

arrived; Mark and I went from elation to fear and concern in a split second.

"There is some sort of a mass at the base of his skull—in his brain."

My thoughts screamed at me, "What?"

"It could be the sign of a genetic issue. I want you to come back in eight weeks so I can take another look."

Mark and I were scared stiff. We didn't know what to ask the doctor. He tried to reassure us that it could just be developmental, but we didn't really hear anything after he said the word "mass."

For the next eight weeks we talked to Mark's sister Kathy, who was a nurse. We spent hours reading about possible causes.

The days and nights dragged along as we talked about what ifs. It was the longest eight weeks of our lives. By the time the next visit arrived, we had lost many nights of sleep and had come to realize in a whole new way the immensity of having a child and being responsible for another life.

Mark and I were holding hands tightly as we walked into the office for the second appointment. The doctor had me sit down immediately for the sonogram, and without even speaking he went to the spot he was looking for. He obviously knew we had been extremely worried. It seemed like he wanted to put our minds at ease as quickly as possible, if that was what was going to happen.

We waited for him to say something almost without breathing. He looked up and said, "Everything is okay. It's resolved itself through development."

Silent tears flowed out of my eyes. My shoulders

relaxed, and I felt as though I could breathe again for the first time in eight weeks.

When I was finished with the exam, Mark held me for several minutes. I looked up at him and said, "Connor is going to be okay."

He just held me. I don't think he could speak. We went home exhausted but relieved and, underneath all of the crushing emotion, very happy.

I was a little skeptical about what Mark had said regarding Connor's anger, but I thought that going in and talking to Connor while he slept couldn't possibly *hurt*. And I knew how much Mark cared about Connor.

Connor had been asleep for about an hour, so I slowly opened his door. I tiptoed over to his bed, feeling very silly that I was going to talk to him when he was asleep. But anything was worth trying if it would help him through these feelings he was having.

I leaned close to him and said in a voice just over a whisper, "Your daddy decided to leave because he loved you so much and so *you* could be happy."

I thought for a moment that I needed to say more but I heard, "That's perfect; it's all he needs right now. He will instinctively know the rest."

It seemed that Mark was right. Over the next few days, Connor's anger seemed to begin subsiding. I suppose the words I spoke over him while he was asleep sank into whatever subconscious place was giving rise to his feelings. I felt so grateful for Mark's loving presence and his insight.

COUNSELING

Over the next few months I had several counseling sessions with Sabrina. One day I walked into her office and sat down on the big overstuffed, cuddly couch and looked over at her.

As usual she said, "So, how are you doing?"

"Actually I think I'm doing pretty well. I've had some bumps with the boys and seem to be very busy, but overall I feel pretty good. I'm kind of surprised, really."

"Tell me about being busy."

"Well, I'm helping Jeremy get trained; I feel responsible for making sure that happens correctly. I'm still doing all of the office work for the company. I'm taking care of the boys. I'm exercising more. I joined a gym. I'm trying to make time to see friends a little. I'm starting the probate process for the will. I'm handling our investments as I was before, and I'm running my real estate company."

When I stopped to take a breath, she said, "Okay. So it seems to me that your plate is bigger than this room and is overflowing."

I laughed and realized she was right.

She said, "You are trying to do everything right now."

"Yes."

"Is it helping you cope? Is the *doing* filling up the space of your *feeling*?"

"I guess."

I hadn't really thought about it. I'd always been a go-getter and it just seemed that now I was only able to take on the basics in order to be able to hold everything together.

She said, "It doesn't have to *all* be done right now. You need to feel, too."

She kind of sounded like my mom. I said, "I know. Maybe I should look at what I'm doing and cut out some things that aren't vital right now."

"I'd suggest that. You need time for you. You need time to relax."

During another session I remember her saying, "It's been a few months now; how do you feel when I ask you to consider the possibility of writing a goodbye letter to Mark, in terms of being your partner who is present in your physical life?"

I instantly stiffened as a hard, strong feeling hit my veins; it felt like a mix of anger and denial. I defensively said, "There's no way I could do that now. He isn't gone. I don't feel that I need to say goodbye. Why would I write him a goodbye letter when he is right here with me?"

I don't think I even really heard what she was saying. Still, she looked at me and nodded her head. She said, "When you're ready, it might help give you some closure to the relationship."

I didn't feel that I was ready for that to happen. I felt that I was just starting to get to know the part of him I'd always wanted to be close to. I wondered if there would ever be a time when I would feel ready to write a goodbye letter to him. At the moment it didn't seem feasible. He was with me. He had told me he wasn't going anywhere unless I wanted him to. I didn't want him to go anywhere; I wanted him with me.

Several weeks later my life seemed to be gliding along. When I sat down on the couch Sabrina said, "I need to ask you something."

"Okay."

"What are you doing for yourself?"

I sat there for a long time. I couldn't think of anything in particular. Then I said, "I got a massage the other day. Does that count?"

"Yes, of course. I'm not talking about big things, I'm talking about anything. I have a list here of ideas for people who need to take better care of themselves. Would you like to look at it?"

"Sure!"

I took the paper from her hands and started to go down the list. It was pretty long, and I noticed something strange: I had done almost every single item on it. There were things like "relax in the sunshine," "have a cup of tea," "take a long bath," "exercise in a way you enjoy," "call a friend," "buy something you really like that is affordable for you," "take a minute to just breathe," "get a massage," "read a fun magazine," "see a funny movie," and on and on.

I looked at her and said, "I've done almost all of these things. What does that mean?"

"You have a natural talent for taking care of yourself. You'd be surprised at how many people aren't knowledgeable on that topic. By doing these things you are able to function better for yourself and everyone who is in your life. Keep doing them."

FOURTH OF JULY

Mark's dad and sister, Papa and Aunt Kathy, had been planning to visit us over the Fourth of July weekend. The boys and I were so excited for their trip; it felt like a part of Mark was going to be around. His dad and he were so alike, after all. I couldn't wait for one of Papa's big bear hugs.

They arrived at about dinner time on Friday, and we sat around the dining room table and caught up on each other's lives. The next day I had planned a trip to the zoo for us. We all went and had a great time. On the way home Papa said, "We are going to take off after dinner."

I was crushed. I thought they were going to stay until Sunday afternoon. I looked over at Mark's sister and said, "Why?"

"Dad needs to get back for church and golf tomorrow."

I was so overwhelmed with sadness I couldn't understand it. I guess in some ways it felt like Mark was closer to us when his dad and sister were there. The problem was that I was expecting to have that feeling for longer than it seemed I was now going to.

I said, "Is there any way you could at least stay the night and maybe have breakfast with us in the morning? I told the boys you were going to be here all weekend and that we would go see a parade together."

They discussed the possibility of staying and said they could do that. In the morning we got up and sat around the kitchen table, again sharing our lives. The boys played tricks on Papa and sat on his lap. They were so happy; I didn't want it to end. When Papa and Aunt Kathy got up to go I gave them both hugs. As soon as I let go of Papa, my heart felt heavy in my chest and tears started running down my cheeks and off my chin. It felt as though the Band-Aid of them being there was being ripped off.

I couldn't stop crying. I did my best to look happy and wave when they left, but I was a mess. We watched them go until they were all the way down the block. When I shut the door I crumbled into the nearest chair. It seemed like I had been doing so well, and now this.

The rest of the day was a disaster. I finally stopped crying about the time I finished doing the dishes from breakfast. We were getting ready to go to the neighborhood Fourth of July parade, and I realized we had missed the starting time and it was probably already over. The boys were troupers, but for me it felt like another stab in the gut.

I thought maybe it might help if I went outside and felt the warm air. I walked out on the deck and sat in a chair. It was then that I remembered it was exactly five months since Mark had died. The thought was too much; I knew I had to get away from the house.

The boys and I went to the grocery store to pick up a few things we needed. By then they were tired and acting like normal three- and five-year-olds, but I didn't have the energy to deal with their bickering, and I lost it. I yelled at both of them in the car on the way home—so loud it hurt my throat. Then I felt horrible about that.

A couple of hours later, I remembered we were supposed to go over to my dad's house for a picnic. I also remembered I was supposed to bring an appetizer. I'd completely forgotten, and I felt like an idiot. I'd even been at the grocery store but hadn't gotten anything that would work.

I called and told them I didn't have anything made. They said it was no problem and that we should just come over. I knew I should go and enjoy the day; it was a holiday, a time for friends and family to be together and laugh. But all I could do was think about how our family was ripped apart, never ever to be the same.

While we were driving to Dad's house I started crying again. I called my mom on my cell phone. She talked with me, but nothing she said seemed to help. I couldn't get out of the funk that had started when Mark's dad and sister left.

When I got to my dad's house I talked with my sister-in-law and my stepmom, but nothing they said could break the negativity that had set in on me.

That night I put the boys in bed, walked into my room, curled up in a ball, and cried. It seemed that after all I'd been through that something so small as Papa and Aunt Kathy leaving earlier than I expected shouldn't have had such an effect on me.

I decided that maybe I should just go to bed and start over tomorrow. Instead, however, I decided to write in my journal. I picked up a pen and started to write down how I felt and what had happened during the day. I'd thought I was moving forward and healing so well, yet today felt like a huge step backward. I knew somewhere there had to be some sort of reason for this pain. Today the writing wasn't even helping.

I lay on my bed for a while and realized I felt very alone. My family was supportive, my friends were amazing, and the boys were an absolute gift, but the day was just so painful.

I tried to think of someone whom I could call that would understand. I had already tried with my mom, stepmom, and sister with no results. Then for some reason I thought about David. He'd said I could call about anything. He'd helped me through my fears about Paul. I wondered if maybe he could help me now. I decided to see if Mark had a thought either way.

"David's really good at things like this. Give him a chance."

I hesitated for a moment, thinking I'd be embarrassed to share this day with David. I'd talked with him about business, but this was pretty different. I didn't want to bother him and it was getting late, so I texted him and asked if he was busy.

He immediately responded: "Kind of. Do you need to talk?"

I wrote back, "Yes."

Within ten seconds the phone rang and I heard him say, "Hey, how are you? What's going on?"

For some reason, when I heard his voice and the caring in it, relief swept through my body and the upset from earlier started to ebb.

I told him about Mark's dad and sister leaving earlier than I expected. I told him how hard it was on holidays that were meant for families. I told him how it had been an anniversary of Mark's death and how I'd yelled at the boys. The tears were streaming out of my eyes the whole time. I let it all out until there wasn't anything left.

He just listened until I stopped talking and then he said, "You're a single mom now. I've been a single dad for four years. It's hard; there's no sugarcoating it. Taking care of the boys by yourself will be much harder than it was with Mark there to support you. Don't feel bad about yelling at them. All parents yell at their kids."

I let out a long breath. That may have been the *one* thing that bothered me most about the day, and it was the first thing he addressed.

He continued, "I try not to yell at my son, but sometimes it happens. Kids love us and need us so much that if you tell them you're sorry and say you'll try to communicate better next time, they will forgive you. My son even reminds me later when I get upset that I need to communicate better. We work together as a team."

It was kind of funny having David give me parenting advice. I thought it was great advice, but we had never talked about things like that before.

The next thing he said surprised me even more. "As far as all of the other things you talked about, what do you think is going on? What are you feeling? Do you think you are missing Mark, that you're overwhelmed, or that you're just plain feeling lonely?"

My stomach felt tight when he mentioned all three, so I said, "Honestly it seems like it's a mixture of all three. I think one would be okay, but the mix plus the holiday made me hit a wall."

Then I thought, "Wow, he's asking me about my feelings? I guess Mark was right; David *is* good at this."

We talked a little while longer. He said he was amazed at everything I had done since Mark passed away. We talked about Mark some and how he would have loved to see the boys with their Papa this weekend. We talked about how Mark was probably watching us the whole time. I even started to smile a little.

I told him thanks for all of the positive feedback on what I had been doing. He said, "No problem. If you want to set up a nightly phone call and I can be supportive, gregarious, and funny, let's do it!"

I laughed.

"You know, Jen, you're a very straightforward, logical person, and I'm a touchy-feely guy; we make a pretty good team."

We'd known each other for a while now and I knew a little bit about him. We'd even done real estate deals together, but I'd never thought of us as a team.

When we were saying goodbye he said, "You know I love you and the boys, right?"

I didn't know what to say. My first instinct was that he meant he cared about me deeply because we were friends and I was Mark's wife, but when I hung up, I wondered.

FAMILY

One day on the way home from school we pulled up to the mailboxes and Brannon said, "Mommy, can I get the mail?"

I looked back at him and said, "Sure!" I handed him the key.

I watched him carefully open his door, step down to the sidewalk, and go over to the mailboxes. He had to get up on his tippy toes in order to reach the keyhole. As he turned the key to open the box I had such a feeling of pride. He was getting to be such a big boy, so independent, strong, and confident. He was such a pleasure to watch.

When he pulled out the mail a key dropped to the ground. He said, "Mommy! Mommy! There's a key! Does that mean we have a present?"

"It might. Bring me the mail and then see which box the key is for."

He carefully held the big stack of mail in his hands and handed it to me through the window of the car. Then looked at the key closely.

"Mommy, it has a seven on it."

"Okay, then try to open the big door with the seven." He pushed the key in carefully and turned it. When the door popped open he looked up at me with joy in his eyes. He reached into the larger mailbox, pulled out a brown box, and brought it over to me.

He said, "Is it for me?"

I looked at the label and my heart started pounding hard against my ribs. It was from the people who had created Connor's baby video. They had finished Brannon's and sent it to us.

"Hop in! Let's go home and open it. It's for all of us."

At home, we opened the box. Inside was a video in a container that was completely covered with family photos. Most of them were of Mark and Brannon.

Brannon said, "Mommy! What is it?"

"It's your baby video."

"Can we watch it?"

"Yes!"

I knew there would be a lot of footage of Mark, so I wanted to prepare the boys. We had not watched any videos of him since he had died. I wondered how the boys—and I—would take seeing him so alive.

"Now boys, you know that Daddy will be in this movie, right?" They both got huge smiles on their faces and said, "He will?" I guessed they were okay with it. I put the movie into the player, and we all sat down on the couch. The scene that started took my breath away: it was Mark holding Brannon on the day he was born. It then changed to a clip of him holding Brannon like a little doll and wiggling his feet like he was running down the hill in front of our house. Brannon, Connor, and I were laughing uncontrollably in the video, and we laughed now as we watched it.

As the movie continued I tried to keep an eye on how the boys were reacting. They both were in wonder and mostly smiling. It seemed okay for them to keep watching. I looked back up at the television and saw Mark set down Brannon and look directly into the camera.

What he did next I will never forget. He put his hands on his heart, closed his eyes and then opened them, and put his arms out toward the camera as if he was giving me his heart. At the same time he mouthed the words, "I love you."

I didn't remember shooting that. The tears started to fall from my eyes. I felt empty and filled at the same time. His love was flowing into me in that moment, and I felt guilty that I didn't remember him doing that in person. It made such an impression on me now, but when I'd taken the video I'd taken his expression of love for granted. Now it was everything—it was him. There was my man, telling me he was giving me his heart. I melted. I missed him.

When the video ended I couldn't say anything. The boys were excited and wanted to watch it again. I let them, but I left the room. I didn't need to see it again; that motion and those words were burned into me forever.

While the boys were watching the video I went upstairs to my office, wanting to be alone for a few minutes. When I turned on my computer I saw several unopened emails. I skimmed down the list quickly and noticed one from Mark's sister.

I opened it and read what she said. She was asking me for a copy of the will again. She had asked before, but I had not wanted to give it to her. I knew it was not going to make her happy, since we had chosen to have Mark's stepsister Kathy be the guardian of our children after my brother. I knew his sister would be upset about that.

I picked up the phone and called Kathy.

"Hey, Jen, what's up?"

"She's asking for a copy of the will again."

"Well, if she's going to keep asking, then just send it to her."

"But I don't want her to be hurt."

"It isn't your job to keep her from hurting. It's your job to take care of you and the boys. If she is going to make an issue about it, then just send it to her. I'm okay with it."

"What about the fact that you are the boys' guardian?"

"Well, why did you and Mark make that decision?"

"Mainly because when we wrote our wills, you were married and she wasn't."

"Well then send it to her, and if she asks, then tell her."

We talked a little more and hung up. I sat down at my desk, made a copy of the will, and sent it. I had no idea how she would react. I wondered why she wanted a copy of the will. Mark had left everything to the boys and me, and I'd told her that.

About three days later I got another email from her. It started out with the words, "I guess I wasn't the sister to Mark that I thought I was."

I hesitated to read farther. I knew she was hurting tremendously, but I couldn't handle having to take on someone else's hurt right now. I felt my hands were so full with our lives that it was impossible. However, I kept reading.

She went on to say how she was devastated that we didn't choose her as the guardian for our kids.

I almost decided to ignore the email, but instead wrote back simply, "you were not married when we created the will. That's why we made our decision. I'm sorry it hurt you. It wasn't meant to do that."

About a week later I got an email from her saying, "Thank you for telling me why you made the decision. I am doing much better now. Also, there was something I wanted to talk to you about. My husband and I are thinking of buying a house. Is there any way you could help us?"

As I read the email I wondered. Was she asking me for help doing the real estate transaction, was she asking me for money, or was it something else? I had no idea.

If she was asking me for help on the real estate deal, there was no way I had time for that. I hadn't had time to think about real estate since Mark had died and she didn't even live in our city. As far as the money question went, I had enough money to help people if they were in a very bad situation and didn't have any other alternatives, but I had to raise my kids and get them through college on my own now. I couldn't help her with buying a house. But I didn't answer the email because I didn't know what to say.

A few days later I noticed she had written to me again. This time the email said, "Disregard the last email. We are not going to buy a house right now."

I was relieved that I didn't have to address that issue. I hoped she was doing ok. I knew loosing her brother had really affected her and I didn't want to make anything harder on her than it already was.

The next week Mark's mom and stepdad were coming to visit us. I was hoping it would be a nice visit with lots of grandparent quality time with the boys. They got into town on Friday afternoon and we went to dinner that night.

When the boys were playing on the playground at the restaurant, Mark's stepdad said, "Jen, I don't know if you know, but when Mark was alive he told us that we would never have to worry about money. I don't know exactly what he meant, but I just wanted you to know."

I didn't know what to say. I thought about it for a minute and said, "Mark isn't here anymore. I am in a different situation than I was before. I don't know what's going to happen with the company. I don't know what I may need to do with the boys if they ever have a genetic issue. I have no way of guaranteeing I can provide for you."

I was hoping the words came out right, but I felt as though I was stumbling hard. I felt pressure, guilt, confusion, anger, sadness, and frustration all at the same time. I just wanted to disappear.

The next morning I woke up and went out to feed Dallas. When I opened the door I noticed that part of the fence looked broken. As I was walking over to take a closer look, I realized there was half of a dead squirrel on the ground. I started to gag. It was disgusting.

I kept walking over to the fence and realized that two of the wooden slats were torn down. What was going on? I went back in the house and asked Mark's stepdad if he would help me with the fence. He said yes. Then I went to take care of the squirrel. I put it in a bag and threw it in the trash. I so wished Mark was there to help.

When I walked back into the house my cell phone rang, but it stopped mid-ring. I picked it up to look at the screen; it was black. I tried to turn it on and off, but nothing happened.

I sank onto the couch and put my head in my hands. Why were these bad things happening? I decided to go for a swim to clear my head. I asked Mark's mom and stepdad if they would watch the boys for a bit, and then I headed to the pool.

As I was gliding through the water taking deep breaths, I had the thought that maybe something I was doing or thinking was creating this chaos. I kept swimming without stopping, lap after lap, as I cleaned out the junk from my mind and body. I began to wonder if things were going wrong because I'd been unwilling to completely address the issue about money the night before with Mark's parents.

I decided right then that I would talk with them before they left. I didn't want there to be any bad feelings between us; their relationship with the boys was too important.

When I got home I made pancakes and we had breakfast together. I knew they were going to head home soon, so I put the boys in front of the television upstairs and came down to talk. Both

Mark's mom and stepdad were sitting in the living room when I walked in.

I sat down on the couch, looked at them, and said, "I need to talk to you guys about something. I know you're scared right now. I realize that Mark and I were maybe your backstop for money and support. The thing is, I need you to be open with me. Mark isn't here anymore, and you will have to talk with me. I'm really interested in making sure you are both a part of our lives." I seemed to have their undivided attention, so I kept going. "I am willing to help you, but I need you to tell me what you need, when you need it, and why you need it."

Mark's stepdad said, "That sounds good. I guess we just didn't know how to bring it up."

"How are you doing right now?" I asked.

"We're okay. We are making ends meet."

"Well, alright. Why don't you just keep me a little more informed, and when things come up we can talk about them."

He said, "That works for us."

I took a deep breath, settled more into the couch, and said, "You know, I don't intend to desert you guys just because Mark is gone. I think of you as my parents and you will always be the boys' grandparents, and that will never change."

When I looked at both of them I could tell they were more relaxed. I think maybe this was what they had been more worried about than money—that they wouldn't be considered part of the family or that we wouldn't continue to have them in our lives. I knew in my heart that was the furthest thing from the truth.

THE RING

A few weeks later I dropped off the boys at school, and as I drove away I started to cry. This was not an unusual experience, but this day it seemed worse than normal.

That morning at breakfast Brannon had looked at my wedding ring and then at me and said, "Mommy, I don't want you to wear that ring anymore."

I was so surprised that I didn't say anything back. But now that I was alone, the conversation and idea pushed into me, forming a pressure that I was resisting.

I believed I was doing well, considering that I had lost my husband a few months ago. But sometimes I still felt very alone and that nobody could possibly understand what I was going through. It seemed to me that if I took my wedding ring off, I wouldn't have any physical connection left with Mark.

At the same time I wondered if Brannon was having a hard time looking at the ring and twirling it when I read to him. I imagined it might be reminding him of Mark and the loss of his daddy. I didn't want him to suffer.

I felt torn. I wanted the ring on my finger for a connection, but I wanted to take it off for Brannon. I didn't know the right thing to do. My mind was spinning.

And then I heard, "Sweetie. Sweetie. There's no way you will ever *not* have a connection with me unless that's what you want."

I wiped my eyes hard with the back of my hand and said, "How are you?"

It seemed like a silly question, but it's what I had always asked him when he had been there, and it was a difficult habit to break.

"You don't ever have to ask me that again. I am. That's all. In your terms I'm always experiencing bliss. I'll always be as well as you could possibly imagine. The real question is, how are you?"

"Sometimes I'm great; sometimes I'm sad, scared, and lonely. Right now I feel like a mess. I don't want to stop wearing my wedding ring, but Brannon asked me to. I don't know what to do with that. What should I do?"

"It's only a ring. Why don't you try taking it off and see how it goes? Brannon will be okay either way, and I'm not going anywhere."

I was surprised at his answer. But when I heard it, a thought fell into my mind. Before Mark had died I was planning on wearing the ring forever, but now at times it felt like a lie. I wasn't married anymore. Maybe the decision was not only about Brannon. Maybe I needed to see what it felt like to not wear the ring. But was I really ready to take it off?

When I got home I went up to my room and stood by my dresser. I slowly slid the ring off my finger and set it in my jewelry box. It felt as if I had torn a part of my body off. I'd worn that ring almost every single day for close to nine years.

I closed the lid to the jewelry box and stood there for a few minutes, holding onto the dresser.

In some ways it felt sad, as if I were closing the door to a time in my life that would never return. I was surprised, though, that after a few moments it also felt a little liberating, as if there was something out there that was going to be new and exciting. I was stunned; I didn't expect the second part of that. I even started to feel a little guilty.

I heard, "It's okay, right?"

"For some reason it is," I said.

"I'm so happy. I want nothing more than for you to live your life completely. Holding on to what we had before is not going to be helpful for you. There is nothing to feel guilty about."

I didn't understand why he was saying these things. Didn't he want people to know we'd been married?

He said, "I'm the same but I'm also different. When I was there with you I had a lifetime of junk stuck on me. It made me who I was as a human. Now I'm free of that; I see clearly. I understand—I know. Life is meant to be lived in each moment. You need to live in the moment—not in the past, not in the supposed, lost future. You're an amazing person and your life is incredible; know that. You are supposed to be astoundingly happy. Don't grieve; *live*."

Somewhere deep down I knew there was a seed of truth in what he was saying. However, not wearing my wedding ring felt like a very big step, and it seemed a little too soon. I didn't know if I wanted to take that step just yet. However, I decided to trust him. I took a deep breath, turned, and walked out of the room.

PROBATE

Over the last few months I'd been attempting to figure out the tangled web of probate law and the court system in our state. Mark had a will, but there were some complicated items in it that I was unsure about.

I met with five different attorneys in less than six weeks. Each one had said something different, and one asked for a huge retainer. As far as I could tell, none of the attorneys had any compassion for me and they didn't care about my situation at all. I didn't know where to turn next.

One day, as I drove away from a particularly difficult attorney meeting where I had walked out nearly in tears, I realized I was starving. I was downtown near a popular local health food store that had an incredible café outside, so I parked and went in.

As I got in line I saw someone in my periphery wave slightly. It was David, who was having lunch with someone I didn't know. He stood up and walked over to me.

"Hey, how's it going?"

"Not so great." My voice cracked a little.

"Why don't you get your food and come over and talk? We're done eating and my friend is leaving."

I was embarrassed to feel so fragile. I got my food and walked over to his table, trying to compose myself.

"Okay, tell me everything," David said. "What's going on?"

I looked over at him and realized he really wanted to know. "I've met with five attorneys about probating the will, and none of them are working out. I think it's me."

"I doubt it," he said.

Those three small words were such a relief. I told him about the meetings and what had happened. He said, "Do you want some ideas?"

"Yes, absolutely."

"Okay. I've been reading a book that might be really good for you to read right now. And I also do yoga; it might be something you might want to try."

I didn't know what to say. Those were not the kinds of ideas I thought he would be giving me; I was expecting a referral to an attorney.

"The book is called *A New Earth*, and it's by Eckhart Tolle."

I said, "I started that book about a year ago, but it was very technical and I couldn't finish it."

"Well, there are some things in it that have helped me cope with Mark's death and with life in general. You might try it again."

"Okay, I'll see. Thanks."

"I've been doing yoga for several years now," he went on. "My ex-wife is an instructor, and it's something that has helped me deal with many issues. It's been very centering. Yoga gives me an inner sense of strength that nothing else has ever come close to. You should come to a class sometime."

I was a little skeptical. I had things in my life that aided my strength: I had swimming, the boys, work, my family, and friends. I didn't think stretching into funny postures would help me with inner strength. But I told him I might try it.

When I finished eating we were walking out to our cars. On the way out he said, "Well, I'm sure you have a big week coming up. Go get 'em!"

When I heard those words I felt exhaustion spread through my bones. I looked over at him and said, "All I really want to do is take a vacation."

He stopped walking and looked at me. "Then you should. I bet there is nothing on your plate that can't wait a week."

I hadn't thought of it that way before. I was completely worn out from everything I'd been trying to handle. What would happen if I took a vacation? Could I pull it off? I let out a sigh and said, "That would be heaven."

I looked at him. "I am so glad I ran into you. It feels nice to have someone care. Thanks for helping me so much with getting Jeremy trained, with Paul, with the attorneys, and even with the kids. Thanks for being there for me at a very difficult time in my life. You have made many things a lot easier."

"That makes me feel great. You may not believe it, but I get as much out of talking with you as you get out of it. You're doing an amazing job with everything. You're an inspiration. If you *ever* need to talk about anything at all just call me, really. And let's do a yoga class together soon."

While I was driving home I realized that in a way I *was* going on a vacation soon. I had planned a trip to California for my cousin's wedding months before, and it was coming up in a couple of weeks. I was going to get a break.

THE FLIGHT

While I packed up the boys for our trip to California, I felt nervous about traveling by myself with them. It was a lot of work just getting them and the luggage out of the house, let alone through an airport and all the way to my parents' house, by myself. Connor and Brannon were full of energy and never stood still. I worried about keeping them safe.

However, there was something else I was also a little afraid of: How would I feel at a wedding? It was the first wedding I would attend since mine and Mark's, and I didn't know whether I'd be reminded of our wedding and feel horrible, or if seeing the bride and groom would make me feel sad.

While we were on the airplane I turned on a movie for the boys to watch. Then I got out my computer to do some writing. While I was waiting for it to boot up I closed my eyes, leaned back against the headrest, and became still.

As I was resting, I wondered if Mark was with us. As usual I heard, "Of course." I felt his smile. I kept my eyes closed and smiled, too.

He said, "How are you?"

"I'm doing pretty well. I'm a little surprised at how well, actually."

"Awesome. Then do you want to have some fun?"

I chuckled, thinking that if he'd said that while he was sitting next to me on an airplane while he was alive he'd have been teasing me, and I'd have blushed.

"Sure. What do you have in mind?"

"I thought it might be fun to talk about life."

He had my attention.

He said, "You're going on a trip and are going to have some free time, so I thought we might be able to discuss some things that might come in handy while you're *there*."

I wondered if he meant *there* in California or *there*, as in here on earth.

"Yes."

Ahh. "I guess we could do that," I said.

He said, "What's the difference between you and me?"

"What do you mean?"

"What is the literal difference, right now, between you and me?"

"Literally?"

"Yes, just literally. Think basic, simple, one thing."

"Well, I guess you are there and I am here."

"Almost. I'm actually there *and* here, and so are you."

I wasn't ready to try to wrap my head around that, so I let it go. I thought for a minute longer.

"Keep thinking; you're close."

I suddenly knew the answer. "You don't have a body, and I do!"

"Yes!"

"Okay, but what's the point?"

"Listen closely. If you take this in and live it, it has the ability to change your life and all of the lives you touch. It will *free* you."

I couldn't imagine what he was going to say, but I was all ears.

"The entire point of having a body and being alive on earth is to *experience your body*."

I didn't really get what he was saying until he added, "The only thing that you need to do is see, smell, touch, taste, listen, and feel your feelings. That's all. Do those things and you *will* live an extraordinary life. It's that simple.

"Everyone has the key to bliss with them at all times. Most just don't know how to turn it in order to unlock the door. The mistake most people make is to think life has to be complicated; it doesn't. Just see, smell, touch, taste, listen, and feel your feelings."

"That seems so shallow. Isn't there more to being here? It seems too simple. Why would there be so much focus, drive, and competition in the world as it pertains to our careers and paths?"

"Why don't you try it and see what happens?"

"Well, I can do that."

I sat in the chair with my eyes closed and felt the seat behind my back, the armrests, and Connor's arm. I felt my own feet in my shoes. I smelled the dry, cool air. I tasted the gum in my mouth. I opened my eyes and looked around at all of the people and the airplane. I listened to people talking, the hum of the airplane, and the boys breathing next to me.

A huge wave of emotion rushed through my heart. Life was SO ALIVE! It was overwhelming. I felt held by the world around me; I felt connected. This was incredible! Only moments before I would have said nothing special was going on around me. I would have said I felt alone.

Tears started to run down my face—tears of relief. I didn't have to *think* all the time. I didn't have to be *doing* something all of the time. Life was meant to be experienced. The thinking and doing were just extra work that got in the way of experiencing. Tension, worry, and fear were washing off me in waves.

I closed my eyes and focused on Mark. "My God, thank you."

He said, "Now you can *really* live."

THE DECK

During the week we spent at my mom's house you couldn't have handpicked better weather. It was eighty degrees and sunny, with fluffy, white clouds in the sky. There was a gentle breeze blowing through the huge pine trees, making a soft, shuffling sound that relaxed my soul. Most days I spent a few hours out on the deck, drinking lemonade and reading *A New Earth*.

I also took Mark's conversation to heart and spent time watching the huge pine trees sway very gently with the breeze blowing through them. I listened to the blue jays caw at each other. I watched and listened to the dozens of hummingbirds that flew around the deck, dizzyingly vying for the sugar water my parents put out for them. I felt the sun on my face and focused on what my body was telling me when I had different emotions.

Between focusing on my senses and reading, I realized that every single thing in my life was exactly as it was supposed to be. I found it strange to know this for sure in every cell of my body, especially since my husband had passed away just a few months before. It seemed impossible, yet it was true.

Several parts of *A New Earth* gave me insights into my situation. But the one that struck me the most was when the author talked about how people handle the death of a loved one. He said you have two choices; you can either resist what has happened or yield to what has happened.

He went on to say that if you choose to resist, then your life will be difficult and full of pain. But that if you choose to yield, you will become more conscious, that circumstances and people in your life will become helpful and cooperative and positive coincidences will happen.

When I thought back over the last few months, I started to see a trend. Whenever I was fighting what was happening in my life it became more difficult, such as when I'd been scared about taking care of the company before Jeremy arrived. As a result, Paul came in and was not helpful.

I remembered how angry I'd been while resisting the idea that there was a reason for Mark's death. I also recalled the relief that came when I began to accept it and yielded to the information I was given.

I also thought about how incredible our neighbors and family had been when I let life flow and didn't try to control what was happening. The first few days after Mark had passed away had been a miracle. And at the same time I'd been so exhausted that I'd had no other *choice* but to yield. It made me wonder if I had to be a bit broken down or shocked out of reality to truly yield, or if it was possible to learn this without the constraints of circumstance.

I wondered if I'd be able to yield more and resist less in my life. Sometimes it seemed effortless, and at other times it seemed extremely difficult to let go. Having the knowledge was a start; learning to use it on a regular basis was the challenge of a lifetime.

~

The next day I rode to the wedding with my sister LeeAnne, and the boys rode with my parents. Lee and I spent the time talking, listening to fun music, telling stories, and laughing. So far, so good. But we weren't at the wedding yet.

When we parked the car I had to sit for a minute and take a few breaths. I looked back to my parents' car behind us, then walked over to it. I took the boys' hands and went inside. I sat down in the back row with Connor and Brannon. They were a little wiggly, but for the most part they were behaving like angels.

As my cousin walked out in her wedding gown, I could feel the tears well up in my eyes. I took a deep breath and tried to feel exactly what was going on. I looked back up at her and then down the aisle at her soon-to-be groom. They were both smiling ear to ear. Her eyes were sparkling and her smile was infectious! I immediately felt honored to be in the presence of both of them and to be able to witness the kind of exquisite joy they were experiencing. It was an intoxicating gift.

I realized my tears were not of sadness, as I had feared, but of joy. I hugged the boys close to me and watched as two people joined together for a lifetime of mysteries, challenges, excitement, and love.

At the end of the ceremony the minister said, "You may now kiss the bride." The groom took her in his arms, dipped her, and kissed her like there wasn't anyone around. I think I even saw my grandmother blush and cover her eyes. However, I think she was also smiling.

After the wedding my sister and I drove back to my parents' house. During the drive I was thinking about my marriage and said, "You know, there is only one thing I would have changed about my marriage to Mark if I could."

"Really, only one?"

"Yes. I would have worried less. Every time I worried about anything it was a waste of time. Life was exactly how it was supposed to be, and worrying only made things more difficult."

She glanced over and said, "That's such a hard thing to do, especially with kids. I'm always worried for them even though I don't have any of my own. Just being Auntie Lee makes me very worried sometimes."

"I know. But when Mark died it seemed like my fear of something bad happening went away for the most part. I realized that no matter how much I worried about anything, it didn't stop my worst nightmare from happening. So, what was the use?"

She looked a little skeptical, but I continued. "I'm not saying to not be careful or not take care of life. I'm just saying I worried too much. I could have lived the same life but thrown out the worry, and everyone would have been happier, especially me."

She said, "It sounds great, but I wonder if it works in practice?"

"Well, now when I start to worry I've started to try to breathe more and notice the world around me, rather than get stuck in the thoughts spinning in my head," I said. "It seems like my head clears. When the worry goes away I am more able to observe rather than *attempt* to control, and my whole body relaxes. It feels better and seems to make others around me feel better too.

"It probably isn't for everyone; it's just something I've noticed that has changed for me since Mark died."

She said, "I bet it creates more space in your life for other feelings—better ones, even.

"Yes, I think it does."

LEEANNE

After we'd been home for a week or so, I found myself thinking about David and how he'd been so supportive over the last few months. Every time I'd needed anything he'd been there for me.

The more I thought of him the more I realized I had some feelings for him that were beyond friendship. When I had this thought, it felt good but also strange. Was it too soon? It felt a little scary and risky to open my heart to anything. But even so, the feelings were there.

A few nights later I was thinking about him and decided I wanted to talk to someone about it. I didn't really know what to think, and I needed to hear what someone else thought.

My sister LeeAnne didn't live in our state so she couldn't tell anyone. She was single, unlike most of my family and friends, but most of all she was exciting, loving, caring, and fun all wrapped into one package. Maybe she would give me some words of advice or at least just listen and be neutral.

When she answered the phone she said, "Hey, Sis!"

Ahh . . . LeeAnne. I was definitely calling the right person. I was still a little nervous about what she would think, however.

We caught up on the last week, and then I hesitated for a moment. I wasn't sure how to bring up David. There wasn't really any way to sugarcoat it, so I said, "What would you think if I told you I might have feelings for a man?"

For the first time that I could remember, LeeAnne didn't respond. The line was quiet for several seconds, and I wondered if our call had been interrupted or dropped.

"Lee?"

"Sorry. I was crying."

She was crying? I was even more nervous now. Did she think it was too early, or wrong? Maybe she was just sad that I wasn't with Mark anymore.

Finally, she said, "Don't worry. I'm happy—*so* happy. I'd been worried that after Mark you might never feel that way about someone again. Please, go on."

I was speechless. That was not the response I was expecting. I smiled.

"Do you remember David from the memorial service? He was the one who read four pages that he wrote about Mark."

"Are you kidding? Of course I remember him! He was the tall, dark, and handsome one who told the great jokes and talked about Mark as if he was the person he most respected on this earth, right?"

"Yeah. That's him."

"That's great! Do you have a plan to get him in the sack?"

I laughed out loud. *There* was my sister. "It's not really like that. Plus I don't even know how he feels."

"Well, how do *you* feel?"

"I'm not completely sure. I know I like being around him, and he has really helped me with a lot of things over the past months. But the feelings are kind of new."

"Well, it sounds great to me. Make sure you keep me in the loop on everything."

"I'll do that. Thanks. I didn't know how you would react."

"What do you mean?"

"Well, it's a little soon, isn't it?"

"I don't think so. I have a friend who's been dating a man who lost his wife. They met two months after she died. They've been together for two years and are doing great. You're strong and alive, and Mark isn't here anymore. Jen, he would want you to be happy. We all want you to be happy."

As I heard her say those words, tears of relief started to sting the corners of my eyes; I couldn't hold them in. It was as if the ball of worry in the pit of my stomach was melting. I didn't realize how concerned I had been about what people would think. Leave it to my sister to say just the right thing.

YOGA

One day the next week, I decided to head over to a yoga class with David. When I was at home getting dressed for the class, I started to feel a little nervous. I'd been looking forward to trying his class, but this was a different feeling than looking forward to learning something new. I realized I was *really* looking forward to seeing David.

During my counseling session earlier that day, I couldn't focus. I told Sabrina I was going to yoga with a friend. She said yoga would be a fantastic idea for me right now. I looked down at the floor and then said, "Well, I'm also excited to see the friend who invited me—and it's a man."

I held my breath when I looked up at her.

She stopped writing. "Is that so?" She smiled. "Do you want to tell me anything else?"

"Well, I'm kind of surprised I might be excited to see a man right now. It seems like in some ways it hasn't been that long since Mark has been gone."

I was testing the water with her on this, just as I had with Lee-Anne.

"Well, how do you feel about that?"

"Honestly, really good."

"I'd say that's a good sign," she said. "You seem to be doing very well with all of the other aspects of your life right now. I don't see why you couldn't enjoy some male companionship, too."

I laughed; she sounded so formal.

"What's the laugh about?"

"I'm actually really nervous. I haven't felt this way in a long time about a man. I'm surprised it's about someone I've known for years and didn't feel that way about before."

"You look happy, maybe even more than happy. Are you?"

"Yes."

"Well, there you have it. That's what's important."

I loved Sabrina; she was so real, direct, honest, understanding, and non-judgmental—the best!

On the drive over to yoga I felt a little silly. I didn't know if David had any feelings for me other than friendship, but here I was like a sixteen-year-old, with butterflies in my stomach. When I entered the lobby I had to register at the counter. David walked in and saw me.

"Hey! I'm glad you came."

I smiled, and my stomach went into my throat. I hadn't noticed how really handsome he was. But this time I did, and my voice wouldn't work. He had dark hair, dark eyes, a toned body, and a great smile. Oh no! What was I going to do with these feelings?

"The room for our class is right over there," he said. "I'll meet you inside when you're done registering."

All during the class I tried to pay attention to what the instructor was saying, because the yoga was pretty advanced. Luckily I was able to fall back on my athleticism from swimming, but it was still difficult for me to follow. When the class did a headstand, I knew that was beyond my capabilities, so I rested and watched. At one point David and I stood facing each other in a pose; he looked me in the eyes and smiled. I smiled back.

At the end of the class we talked for a few minutes. He asked if I liked yoga and if I was going to come again.

"I am pretty sure I will. Let me go see how much it costs."

When I went over to find out about the prices, David went and talked with some of his friends. I hoped he wasn't going to leave before I had a chance to talk with him some more.

I was relieved when he finished with them and came back over. He asked how my week had been. I told him what I'd been doing and asked him the same thing.

He got a serious look on his face and said, "My mom is in a coma."

My mouth dropped open. I reached over, put my hand on his arm, and said, "I'm so sorry. When did this happen?"

"She went into it three days ago. I'm on my way to visit her right now. The doctors aren't sure if she's going to make it."

It seemed that he was trying to be strong and very matter-of-fact. I wondered if he was partly trying to protect me; he probably thought talking about a possible death would upset me. My only thoughts were about him, though. I wondered how this would affect his life and if he was ready for her death if it happened.

"I hope you're doing okay," I told him. "If there's anything at all I can do, please let me know."

"I will. I'd better get going."

The conversation made me realize I cared about David. He had been the one to help me all along, but now I had an overwhelming urge to help him. I knew if his mom died he'd be going through a lot of emotional and difficult times. I felt some of his pain.

MARK

Over the next few weeks I didn't hear much from David. He was driving three hours most days to be with his mom and family while she hung on. One day I opened up my email and saw that he had written. In the message he said that his mom had passed and that everything was okay. He mentioned it was a little difficult working closely with a large family to plan a service. I knew what he meant; the number of decisions that needed to be made quickly had been overwhelming for me. I remembered only too well.

During this time when David was less present in my life I realized I had some deeper feelings for him. I thought about him almost every day and hoped he was getting along okay with the process of losing someone he was close to.

At one point I wondered what Mark might think of this new development in my heart. It had been a few weeks since I'd talked to him.

Before I even formed a question in my mind I heard, "I think it's perfect."

"Really?"

"Absolutely. When I was there, David and I went out on the town when we worked together, but I didn't know the real him."

When he said that, it made me wonder if Mark knew David

better now in the same way he seemed to know me better. If he did, I wondered what he knew.

He said, "David is a wonderful man, and he has deep feelings for you and the boys."

I almost laughed, partly from disbelief and partly from relief. "But he's scared."

"Scared . . . of what?"

Mark said, "David's been hurt in the past. These feelings he has for you tend to scare him a little bit."

I didn't believe what I was hearing. My dead husband was telling me about a man I had feelings for who hadn't even told me these things himself. It didn't seem possible, so I changed the subject back to my original thought.

"Are you really okay with these feelings I have?"

"I think you should be open to getting to know him. He has some characteristics you really love, some I didn't even have. He's able to be completely honest about himself and his feelings when he wants to. I know you appreciate that. But there's one more reason why I think it's a good idea to have him in your life."

I wondered what in the world he was going to say next.

"He loves the boys almost as much as I do."

I was taken aback at Mark's words. But then I thought back to when David had said that he loved the boys and me. I knew he meant it, then and now.

⁓

That night I went downstairs and pulled out some old photo albums. I hadn't done that in a long time; I'd been scared to look at some of the memories so clearly.

The first book was from our honeymoon. I took a deep breath and looked closely at our faces. Mark and I were so wide-eyed and happy. Our whole lives were in front of us. I remembered how exciting that felt.

Then I saw a picture of Mark driving the Jeep we had rented. His hair was flying around, and he was smiling from ear to ear. I remembered I'd taken that picture of him right after we had our crazy adventure, the one we'd laughed about at lunch the day before he died.

It was our fourth day in Kauai, and we'd set out to find somewhere to snorkel. We'd come to the end of the main road and had seen a sign that said "beach." So we grabbed our equipment and jumped out to go explore.

When we got down to the water we saw some people snorkeling in a big cove. As we were sitting down to put our fins on, I noticed there was a bit of a current flowing through the cove from right to left. I'd grown up in southern California at the beach. I knew that even though the ocean was beautiful that the water could be deceivingly dangerous.

I thought maybe it would be a little rough for Mark on the left side of the cove. Though he was very tall and strong, he was not nearly the swimmer I was. I tapped him on the arm, pointed to the left, and said, "I think we should avoid that side of the cove." He nodded.

As we were snorkeling, we became entranced with our surroundings. After a few minutes I stopped and looked up. We had quickly been moved to the left side by the current. I reached over and touched Mark to tell him we needed to swim back toward the other side.

Just as my hand brushed his arm, he was pulled

into an even stronger current. Within three seconds he was twenty feet away from me. I saw him lift his head, his eyes open wide. I yelled at him to stand up; it was only about five feet deep where he was, but he couldn't hear me, and within seconds he was in a deeper area and couldn't reach the bottom.

He started swimming as hard as he could toward me. I knew he needed some help, but there wasn't anyone near us. I swam over to him as fast as I could and reached out to hold his arm.

We were still moving out to sea very quickly. I looked around and realized that on one side of us was a wall of sharp coral and on the other side there were jagged rocks. Usually when you are stuck in a strong current you swim parallel to shore, but in this case that option offered the very real prospect of getting hurt very badly.

I pulled the snorkel out of my mouth and said, "It's okay. Just put your head down and kick as hard as you can. I'll make sure we go in the right direction." He looked like he didn't believe me, but he did it anyway. I stayed next to him and guided him, swimming as hard as I could while he used all of his strength to move forward. It took us about five or six minutes to make up the few seconds of distance we had lost.

We finally got to a point where we could stand up without being dragged backward. By the time we took our masks off we were both panting so hard we couldn't speak. We trudged up on to the beach and sat down heavily on our towels. When he finally caught his breath, Mark said, "That was interesting. You almost lost me on our honeymoon. How would you explain that to the family?" Then he grinned. I had trouble smiling. It didn't seem funny at all.

We sat there for a while, watching the waves and people in the water. Finally we stood up and headed back to the car. As we were walking past the car next to our Jeep, we noticed a sign that said, "WARNING! RIPTIDE!"

We turned toward each other and laughed out loud, a deep, long laugh of relief and gratitude.

For a moment I was a little dazed with the memory. Was this experience the reason Mark knew what would happen to Brannon in Cozumel? Maybe he knew there would be another, deadlier riptide. The idea sat heavy on my mind. I had to turn the page.

As I flipped through the pictures, I came across one of Mark holding a newborn Connor in his arms on the day our son was born. Pain pressed into my heart. Mark looked so proud, so gentle, so warm and loving. God, how could he be ripped out of the boys lives so fast? I couldn't look at any more memories. I closed the album and went up to bed.

That night I had a dream about Mark. In the dream the boys and I were playing together in the living room, when suddenly the doorbell rang. I told Connor to go see who was at the door. The next thing I heard was, "Daddy!"

I stood up and walked to the door to see Mark standing there. He knew he had come back to life, the boys knew he had, and I knew he had, too. There was no explanation of why or how, just that it was.

In the dream my heart felt heavy, and I contemplated that feeling during the dream. I looked over at the boys, and they were overjoyed. But for some reason I wasn't. I knew I had to act happy that he was home. I put on a smile and watched the boys and Mark rejoice at being together. I, however, was in shock. It was at that moment I woke up.

During the blurry time between deep sleep and feeling truly awake, I felt a huge wave of guilt wash over me. As the fog of sleep lifted, I opened my eyes and looked around the room, and reality sank in. I saw the picture of Mark and me next to my bed and all of our things, and I rolled into a ball and hugged my knees. I knew without a doubt that if Mark had shown up and this was all a mistake that I would have been filled with joy.

Even though I knew the truth, in the back of my mind I wondered if there was a reason why I'd had those feelings in the dream.

REMEMBER

At the dinner table, I savored the few moments of silence as I peeked over at Brannon. Then I turned and saw that Connor was counting to five on his fingers. When he got there he said, "Okay. Five seconds is over."

We had started doing what we called "five seconds" at Thanksgiving the year before. As a family, we held hands before each meal and were quiet for five seconds. Then we let go and took turns, starting with the youngest, and said what we were thankful for. I liked it so much the first time we tried it that I'd continued the tradition every day.

We didn't even miss a day when Mark had died. Two days after Mark had passed away, Brannon had said, "I'm thankful that Daddy is in heaven."

Today Brannon chimed in with, "I'm thankful that my favorite color is turquoise!"

I looked over at him and said, "Turquoise?"

He'd loved bright pink before but had switched immediately to green the day Mark died; green had been Mark's favorite color. This was the first I'd heard of anything different.

"Yep! Do you know what colors make turquoise, Mommy?"

"I think so, but why don't you tell me?"

He smiled. "Green . . . and BLUE!"

I smiled, too. He knew my favorite color was blue. Maybe he was starting to let go just a little.

Then Connor said, "I'm thankful we are going to Florida in a few weeks!"

Yesterday I'd told the boys I'd planned a trip for the three of us to Florida. I was very excited, too. It felt like the blazing of a new trail for our family.

That night I was getting ready for bed and Brannon was taking a shower in my bathroom. I watched him open the shampoo bottle, squeeze out the shampoo, and put it on his head. It was unbelievable that he was growing up so quickly. He noticed me watching him and smiled. Then he pointed up at the dispenser Mark had installed on the shower wall and said, "Mommy, what's that for?"

"It holds shampoo and soap."

I remembered Mark not only putting it in the shower, but always keeping it full for me. It was a small act of kindness and love that Mark showed me that nobody else knew about.

Brannon said, "Is there any in it now?"

"No."

"Why not?"

"Well, sweetie, Daddy used to open it and fill it up for me. It's kind of hard to do, so I haven't done it."

Then Brannon said something that will be forever burned into my mind.

"Mommy? How can you *remember* that Daddy did that?"

My heart felt as if it was being squeezed up into my throat; he didn't even understand why he couldn't remember the little things about his daddy. Plus it seemed that he now realized that I *could* remember things about Mark.

I turned away; I couldn't look at him for fear of completely breaking down. His innocence and sincerity were pushing a knife into my heart. I wanted him to remember everything; I wanted him to have had decades of memories with his father, not just three-and-a-half short years that seemed to be disappearing. It was so unfair.

I turned toward the sink, covered my head, and pretended I was getting a drink out of the faucet. As I did, my tears spilled down into the drain. I put my arms down on the counter and let the tears flow.

Brannon didn't seem upset, just a little curious.

I didn't want to upset him. But his words touched a part of my heart that was reserved just for him, and I wondered if one day he would understand his loss and feel some of the pain I was feeling.

He didn't say anything when I stood up and wiped my face with a towel. He finished his shower, dried off, and asked if he should get his pajamas on.

"Yes, I'll see you in your room in a minute, okay?"

He nodded his head and ran off.

Sabrina had told me that the boys' memories of Mark would fade earlier and faster than mine, and that in order for them to remember anything about him first-hand they would need to be reminded over and over. Because of his age, this was especially true for Brannon.

I knew with absolute clarity that the biggest responsibility I had was not to *do* the things that Mark used to do but to help the boys remember who Mark was. Brannon had just reminded me of that so clearly.

THE PARK

As I was pouring some salsa out of a jar into my bowl to go with some chips, the phone rang. It was David. He sounded pretty good. I asked if he was doing okay, and he said he was.

He asked if the boys and I wanted to go to the park with him and his son the next day. I told him that would be fantastic.

The next afternoon I got to the park a little early. When David drove up, he got his son out of the car and he ran over to us. All three boys took off like a shot for the playground. After they exhausted themselves on the slides and tunnels, they went over to the wading pool.

David and I sat on the side of the pool next to each other, watching the boys splash to their hearts' content. I could feel my heart beating faster than normal. I asked David how he was doing.

"I'm pretty good. Life is different, though. Everything seems to have shifted. I'm not going around all day being sad or depressed, but it seems the things that used to motivate me no longer do. It feels as if life has a different meaning to it."

I knew exactly what he meant.

He looked over at me. "I guess I'm preaching to the choir on that."

"Yes, even work has taken on a different feel," I agreed. "I am not as driven as I was with some of it, but there are other aspects where I'm actually more driven. When I look at the boys I have a different appreciation for them and life itself. I can't even look at a tree the same way as I did before."

He smiled, then he said something I wasn't expecting. "How long do you think Mark would have waited to date if you had been the one to go?"

I was a little embarrassed and didn't respond right away.

He answered his own question. "I think it would have been a long time. He and I were both raised in the South, and it's probably the 'proper' thing, right?"

My heart sank a little. Was he saying that dating me was something he thought of, but that it would be a long time?

Part of me thought maybe I shouldn't say anything, but instead the embarrassed part of me responded with a silly remark. "Well, actually, he *never* would have dated again, because I told him he couldn't."

When David laughed, I did too, and it took some of the edge off my nervousness.

I remembered my dream from the other night and thought about telling David. He seemed like a safe person, and I was a bit confused about my reaction still.

Before giving myself a chance to overthink it, I said, "I had a dream the other night."

"Really? What was it about?"

I was a bit uncomfortable when I realized I was actually going to tell him. However, I told him about dreaming that Mark had come back to life, and that when I saw him I wasn't happy but had to pretend I was for the boys.

He sat there quietly for a minute. Then he looked over at our three boys who were splashing each other and said, "In some ways you've been given a second chance at love. You and Mark were good together, but you've learned more about yourself, and you can now have as good as or even a better relationship than you had with him. As a matter of fact, you get the opportunity to completely restructure your whole life."

I was worried I'd stick my foot in my mouth with any response that came to mind, so I kept quiet.

David went on, "The other thing I thought of when you were describing the dream is that you might be feeling guilty because you're living on without him and are happy. But don't forget, Jen, he wants you to be happy. You don't have to feel guilty about that."

I knew it was true, but sometimes the idea still felt uncomfortable. Maybe I needed to hear it from someone else in order to start to believe it and live it.

While thinking about what he'd said, I realized I didn't know David personally all that well. I also realized that with every conversation we had, I wanted to know him more. I wondered if he'd let me. I decided to ask him about his ex-wife. I didn't know exactly what had happened and wondered if he'd tell me. I asked him what had happened between them.

"Well, she and I got married right after our son was born. Within three months she told me she wasn't happy and left."

I was shocked! I remembered them splitting up but thought they'd been married and living together for at least a year after their son was born. I mentioned this to him.

"I was so embarrassed when she left me that I didn't tell anyone," he said. "I went into counseling and learned a lot about myself, my patterns, and how they affect other people. I also felt that I began to understand more about why she left and who she was.

"She and I are good friends. I'm sad sometimes, because I think that if we had been back then the people we are now, that we would have stayed together and been happy. But I don't have feelings for her like that anymore."

While I was glad that he had a good relationship with his ex-wife, I was also pleased to hear he wasn't carrying a torch for her.

"Actually I don't think I've told you," David said, "but she's expecting a baby in two weeks and engaged to a wonderful man who loves her and our son."

I looked at him with wide eyes. He hadn't mentioned that his son was going to have a brother. It seemed like a big deal to me, but I didn't say anything.

David looked at his watch and said, "We need to get going. Thanks for meeting us here. It was so good to see you and the boys."

We walked to our cars, and David put his son in his car seat then came over and gave Connor and Brannon each a hug. When he did, he told them both he loved them. Then he turned to me, put his arms around me, and held me.

As I was driving away I remembered what Mark had said about David being hurt.

DOUBT

Over the next few days I mulled over some things that were nagging at me about David. I wondered if maybe my feelings for him came around in order to put a bandage on the pain of Mark's death. I also wondered if I was just projecting feelings I had about Mark onto the next man who came into my life, trying to fill the huge void within me.

I had some fairly strong feelings for David, but maybe they weren't warranted. For one thing, I didn't really know him that well. Was I just making this all up in my mind to avoid the pain of not having Mark around anymore?

I didn't know for sure. It seemed like we enjoyed each other's company and I was definitely attracted to him—but was it real?

And finally, did it even matter what I felt or thought? If he didn't have any feelings like that for me, there wasn't any point in worrying about it anyway. I thought maybe he was just in our lives because he felt obligated. He was the only friend of Mark's who lived in our town; he had a little boy the same age as our kids; he was a nice guy . . . Maybe he just felt it was his job to make sure we were doing okay.

As my mind churned with these ideas I realized I really wanted to know how he felt. It seemed that he liked being around me; it even seemed that he *wanted* to be around me and the boys. That felt good.

I thought about sharing my feelings with him, but the moment I had the thought I felt nervous. Right now it was nice to think that there might be something there; it was nice just to look forward to talking with him and seeing him.

And, truth be told, it was exquisite to feel attracted to him. Even though I was surprised I felt that way so soon, it was reassuring to know I could feel attracted to a man at all again. In many ways, even though my feelings may have been one-sided, I sensed that a part of me was healing.

But, I wondered, was I ready to hear his reaction if his feelings were not similar to mine? Could I handle that right now? Would talking to him about this hurt our friendship? I wasn't sure.

And what about Mark's family? What would they think? Would they be mad at me? Would they be hurt?

As I sat there with these thoughts chasing each other around my mind, I decided to make a call. As the phone was ringing, I realized I was holding my breath. It had been a couple of weeks since I had talked with Mark's dad.

"Hello!"

I let out my breath. Ah . . . Papa. It was so nice to hear his warm, gentle voice.

"Hi, Ray. How are you?"

"Hey, Jen. I'm doing okay. How are you?"

I felt funny just jumping in to the topic of David, especially since Ray knew him. So I told him about the boys and how they were doing. Then I stopped.

"Is there something wrong?" he asked.

"No, there isn't anything wrong. I just wanted to ask you something and I wasn't sure how to say it."

"Okay. Go ahead and ask."

"I was wondering how you'd feel if I wanted to start dating."

"Oh, Jen! That would be okay with me. I don't want you to be alone; I know Mark wouldn't want that either. You know, when Jean passed away I started seeing the woman I'm spending time with within just a few months. I was worried about what people would think, but the ones who cared about me were just fine with it. I even called Mark and asked him how he felt about it."

I remembered that now. Mark had been so worried about his dad after his stepmom had died. But one day Mark had walked into my office with a huge grin on his face and said, "Dad's dating! He just called me to ask if I was okay with that. Can you believe it? Isn't that great?"

"I'd forgotten about that call, Ray. Mark was really happy to hear you were seeing someone. He didn't think it was too soon; he thought it was wonderful."

"Well, so do I. You do what you want, sweetie. I support you."

I told him thanks and hung up. Ray was the only person I thought I needed to talk to. If Mark's dad was okay with me being with someone, then I felt okay about his family. They might not all be happy with me dating, but if Mark's dad was, then it felt right.

The only problem facing me now was that I felt it might be a good idea to know how David felt. I decided to think on that a little while longer.

THE TRUTH

A week or so later David sent me an email. He went into a lot of detail about some of the issues he was dealing with in his life about his mom and asked me a few questions.

I didn't have time to answer everything because I was getting ready to walk out the door to yoga, so I quickly responded and asked if he wanted to grab a bite to eat after class. He said he wasn't going to yoga that night because he was babysitting his son's new baby brother, but asked if I could go to dinner a few days later.

I sent a quick "yes" back and then pretty much ran out the door to make it to class on time. As I was driving to yoga I thought that when we went to dinner it would only be the second time we had ever been alone without the boys. I wondered if an appropriate time might come up for me to talk to him about how I felt.

Just having that thought made me nervous. What if he said, "I only think of you as a friend?" Or "I couldn't see us that way; you will always be Mark's wife in my eyes."

Or—what if he *laughed*? I wasn't sure I could handle that, so I still wasn't sure I could say anything, even if the time seemed right.

The next morning I lay awake in bed. The boys were still sleeping, so I had a few minutes of quiet. I thought about how well I'd been doing over the last few months, a fact I hadn't really shared with anyone except my counselor.

For some reason I still thought I had to answer the question of "How are you doing?" with an "Okay, considering" or something similarly low-key.

I started to feel like a fake, almost like a liar. I'd been hiding behind this façade of sadness for other people. I was acting the way I thought they wanted or expected me to act, not as I felt. The feeling was similar to when I was struggling with wearing my wedding ring. I was putting on a face that wasn't fully who I was.

I decided that as of that day I would start telling people the truth—not some of the truth; not a foggy, gray truth; but the clear truth. The truth was that the boys and I were doing very well most of the time, and sometimes we were fantastic.

I wondered how people would respond to the truth. Would they look at me like I was crazy?

Would they think I was cold or didn't love Mark? Would they just not believe me?

When Jeremy walked in the house for work I had my first chance to test my new resolve. He walked in, and the first thing out of his mouth was, "Hey there, how are you?"

I thought, "Here we go." Then I took a deep breath and said, "Great!"

I held my breath and watched his reaction. He stopped and looked at me, then got a big smile on his face. I saw his shoulders relax and drop. It looked like an actual physical weight had been lifted from him. I was stunned.

He said, "Really?"

"Yes, I'm doing great. Is that okay?"

He walked over to me, wrapped his arms around me, and said, "I'm so glad you are doing well."

Something in my gut relaxed. However, the next thought

made shame burn on my cheeks. How could I have kept this from my brother, the man who had quit his job and moved his family across the country for the boys and me? I felt horrible. I was so sorry I hadn't said anything sooner.

Maybe I hadn't been ready. All I knew was that from then on I was not going to allow fear of what anyone thought about me influence my words or actions. I hadn't realized before that I could actually be hurting someone by doing that, but it was true. By not being absolutely true to myself and showing that to others, I could create pain and worry without even knowing it.

TACOS

Over the next couple of days I debated back and forth in my mind about telling David anything at all about how I felt.

When the day of our dinner arrived, I felt that I'd made peace with the decision to say something. I'd thought about the message I'd taken to heart from reading *A New Earth*, the wisdom of yielding to what *was* rather than fighting to change or move through to something else. I thought this was an area of my life that could use some yielding.

I decided I was strong enough to hear the worst response I could think of David making, so if that was the case it didn't matter what he said. I also had a pretty good feeling our friendship was strong enough to continue even if he didn't have any romantic feelings for me.

On some level it seemed I was lying to him, because he didn't know how I felt. It made my interactions with him feel fake. If nothing else, that had to stop.

That night as I was driving to the restaurant I was so nervous I had to keep rubbing my palms on my legs. I'd decided not to have anything rehearsed, but to just let the night flow and see how it went. I thought that when the time came, the right words would come out.

I parked in the back of the restaurant away from the street, then walked in and looked around. There were a few people sitting at a couple of the tables and some fun eighties music was playing. No David, though. I walked into the waiting area and sat down.

When he walked in, I couldn't stop the smile from spreading across my face. I stood up and walked over to him at the door. He grinned and gave me a hug. He said, "You look like you're doing well."

"I am. How are you?"

"Me too. Let's order; I'm starving."

We ordered our food at the counter and found a table. He said, "So, tell me about how last weekend was. Didn't you say you were going out with some friends?"

"Yes. We went to dinner and then to the grand opening of a sports bar. It was my friend's idea. There was a big fight on television that everyone was watching. I pretty much ignored it; fights aren't really my thing. I had a blast talking to my friends, though."

"Sounds like fun! So, did you meet Mr. Right?"

I was a little taken aback with his comment. I sat there for a second and looked at him, and he smiled. I realized he was teasing me.

"No, not this time. I'm not sure that guys who watch fights are really my type."

He grinned. "That's kind of what I thought."

Our tacos arrived and we dug in. Throughout the meal I never felt it was the right time to say anything. It was easier to just let him take the lead and settle into an easy banter. We were having fun, laughing, and talking about life and the latest lessons we'd learned.

At one point I asked him how his work was going, and he said, "Great! As a matter of fact I have a couple of really big clients who may buy something this year. If they do, I'll make some pretty good money. Do you want to go blow some of it and take the boys to Hawaii?"

I thought, "What did he just say? Did he just say he wanted us to go to Hawaii with him and his son?"

I smiled. "That would be awesome."

"You've been there a few times, right?"

"Yes, my favorite place is Maui. It's so green and lush. When I was there it looked and felt the way I always imagined an idyllic Hawaii should."

I was still getting over the fact that he mentioned going on a trip when he said, "Well, it will be next year. But don't worry, I'm not going anywhere."

With that comment he had my attention. I almost said something, but the waiter came over and interrupted our conversation, asking if we needed anything else.

Then David said, "I probably need to get going."

My heart sank. Maybe the universe was trying to tell me it wasn't time yet. Or maybe I'd let an opportunity go by. I didn't want to rush and tell him what I had to say, but I was sad I hadn't mustered the courage to open my mouth. As we walked out to the car I started to feel even worse.

I even thought, "Mark, what should I do?"

I heard, "Tell him."

When we got to my car David put his arms out and said, "Come here."

I went over to him, and he wrapped his arms around me. He held me and didn't let go. Every cell in my body felt alive. I felt his arms around my back, his chest on mine. I rested my head on his shoulder and still he didn't let go. I completely relaxed into him. After another moment he lifted his head a little and said, "Are you *really* okay?"

When he said that, I wondered if he might have been thinking that the moment was about me missing Mark. I didn't want him to think that, so I said, "Yes, I'm okay."

"Really?"

"Yes, but I was supposed to tell you something tonight and I chickened out," I said.

By the time I got to the words "supposed to" the blood was pounding so loud in my ears I could hardly hear myself speak. But I didn't stop.

He said, "What is it?"

I looked at him closely. I couldn't tell if he knew what it was, so I said, "You know, right?"

He kind of smiled a little and said, "Maybe."

I put my hand on my stomach. I was so nervous, but there was no way now I could *not* tell him.

"No, I don't know," he said. "What is it?"

I took a slow deep breath and forced my mouth to form the words. "I have a big huge crush on you."

He grinned. I was so nervous that I pushed his arm and said, "You knew!"

He smiled more.

I repeated, "You knew, didn't you?"

He didn't say anything. My stomach was in knots.

Finally he leaned back against my car, crossed his arms in front of him, crossed his legs, and said, "Well, there's a possibility it might be mutual. However, I have to be really honest with you right now. I don't see us together like that in the future."

And there it was—the information I wanted so badly, and yet the data itself was not what I had expected or necessarily wanted. My heart sank a little. I didn't say anything.

After a few moments he said, "Are you upset you told me?"

I thought about it for a second, but knew the answer almost instantly. "No, absolutely not."

And I wasn't. No matter what the outcome, I'd wanted to know the truth.

"Are you sure?"

"Yes, I'm sure. If you had said, 'Yuck!' or that you couldn't be my friend anymore I might be upset, but no, I'm not upset that I told you. Thanks for being so honest with me."

"Okay. I've felt like there was something there for a while but just didn't want to hurt our friendship. You and the boys mean the world to me."

"I know. I really do."

I looked at him for a minute, then walked over and gave him a hug and said goodbye. I got in my car and sat there for a moment and held my stomach. My heart was pounding so fast from the rush of adrenaline, but in my gut I could feel there was also sadness. I waited until he left, and then I pulled out of the parking lot.

On the way home I thought about what had happened, about how nervous I'd been to tell David the truth. I felt a little sad about not getting to explore a deeper relationship with him, but for the most part I felt good.

I'd started to invest time and energy into the emotions I had for him, and if they weren't mutual I knew that was the wrong path to go down. I wasn't worried anymore about whether or not he knew, and that was freeing. While I would have enjoyed spending more time with David, after going through the grueling trial of losing Mark it seemed a small hurdle to jump.

I also thought about my life and how much I loved the many parts of it. My work was extremely fulfilling, I was healthy and happy, and the boys and I were going to Florida for a vacation together. I was so excited to spend a whole week with just them.

MOONLIGHT

When we arrived at the resort in Florida on a Saturday afternoon, we walked up the path and through the door of the little cottage we were staying in, right on the beach.

We dropped our bags on the wood floor, and I watched as the boys ran around the house looking in each of the rooms and deciding which bed was whose. Finally they ran outside to explore. I followed them down to the water and swung on a hammock as they made sand castles and splashed each other in the shallow water.

This was *our* time. It felt like heaven.

Each morning we woke up, ate breakfast together out on our front porch, swam for hours in the pool right behind our home-away-from-home, and played on the beach. The boys had the time of their lives.

One of the mornings we were at the pool and Brannon was watching me from the side as I swam a few laps to loosen up. When I stopped he came up to me and said, "What are you doing?"

I told him I was swimming a bunch so I would feel really good.

He said, "I'm going to do that, too!"

He stood up, jumped in, and started swimming toward the deep end. I swam right next to him as he slowly made his way all the way across the pool. When he got to the end I thought he was going to pull himself up to the edge and stop, but instead he took a breath, turned, put his head back in the water, and started back toward the shallow end.

After he had swum five laps without stopping, he poked his head up and said, "I bet you think I'm tired, don't you?"

I laughed and said, "Well, sure I do!"

Then he put his head back down and swam three more laps. As he pulled himself up to sit on the side of the pool, it struck me that he was turning into such a big boy. He was only four, but he was growing into his own little self so quickly.

He looked at me with the most proud smile I'd ever seen on his face. I thought, "How could he have drowned?"

But I knew he'd been in swim lessons for almost a year longer and he was much more capable now. It could have happened. I was so incredibly thankful it didn't.

On the final night of our trip I put the boys in bed, wrote in my diary, and then felt a powerful urge to go outside. I opened the door to our little cabin on the beach and walked out onto the deck overlooking the water. It was dark, but there was a full moon, so I decided not to turn on the light.

I sat down quietly on the double Adirondack chair and thought how nice it would have been to have someone sitting next to me to share the moment. However, it was so beautiful that I quickly forgot about that thought and became entranced by my surroundings.

I looked out at the light from the moon sparkling on the peaks of the waves and listened to the warm breeze brush through the palm trees. As I did, I felt a sadness start to come over me.

I couldn't figure out why. I hadn't had any thoughts about anything that was sad. I wondered if it was because I was alone, but it didn't feel like that was the issue. The sadness continued and even got stronger.

I sat there for a few more minutes, waiting for it to go away. I tried to feel the emotion to see if there was any way I could understand what was causing it. I tried to focus on the beautiful moonlight on the water. Nothing helped.

This was a very strange sensation. I couldn't remember a time in my life where I'd become sad without having a thought that had caused the sadness. And still I was getting more upset each minute. It seemed like darkness was pushing into my vision and heart.

I decided to see if Mark could help me figure out what was going on.

"Do you know why I am so sad?"

"Yes, I do."

"Well, maybe you can help me out here?"

He said, "We never would have come here together."

Oh. I took a deep breath and waited.

He continued, "This is your life, your own path now. Had I stayed, this reality would not have ever come to be."

I thought about what he said and felt that it made some sense, but it didn't feel like that was enough to explain the deep sadness. There had to be something more.

I said, "That isn't everything, is it?"

As I said the words a pang of fear touched my heart. Maybe I didn't want to know. These were very intense feelings I was experiencing.

"No."

I knew I had to know. "What is it?"

"If I had chosen to *stay*, we would have started divorce proceedings today."

A rush of emotion flooded into my throat, veins, bones, and heart. I bent forward and held my hands to my face as the sadness turned into disbelief, pain, and then understanding.

Thoughts flashed through my head. Divorce? Really? In less than a year? How in the world could that be true? Wouldn't we have tried to work on our marriage? Surely we wouldn't have expected ourselves to get over losing Brannon by then? Why would we have already started to get a divorce?

But as unbelievable as it was, it had to be what was going on. The moment I heard the words, my feelings made sense.

The emotions continued to surge through me. As the wind and waves flowed, so did my grief for a loss I had not even experienced. It was as if I were crawling on my knees through a dark cave—alone, cold, and in pain.

Eventually the flood of tears started to help dissipate the sadness. And then after a few more minutes it left, as if it hadn't been there at all. I sat there for a long time breathing in the warm air, feeling my drained body, and looking up at the palm trees swaying in the darkness.

Mark didn't seem to be there anymore. I seemed alone, looking out over the ocean now.

I felt different—somehow cleansed, new, sharp, and alive.

And then a thought hit me with a jolt: "How could I possibly have been feeling what *would have* happened if Mark had decided not to die?" Was that really what I had just experienced? Was that possible?

All I knew was that what Mark had told me had led me out of the cave of darkness I'd been experiencing. I had to believe and trust what I'd heard and felt. There was no measure other than my own experience.

I couldn't go back inside the house right then; my mind and body felt so different. I sat there and breathed in the life around me. I had a clarity that had not existed before. I felt that I could do anything and also that I didn't have to do anything at all. There was space and at the same time fullness.

And then another thought dropped in. I realized that if Mark had stayed or left he would not have been with me physically anymore as of this day.

I had a hard time grasping the truth of that realization.

As the evening melded into my heart, I felt blessed at what a gift Mark had given me, to be experiencing this incredible evening and my trip with the boys rather than the alternative.

I also knew that because of the choice he made he *would* be with me forever. Even though I wasn't speaking with him at this moment, he was with me now in my heart, and I would always love him. I walked back inside where the boys were sleeping soundly and settled into bed.

RAIN

I woke up the morning of our anniversary and instantly got a sick feeling in my stomach. Would people call? Would anyone remember? Did it matter at all to anyone else that this was the day Mark and I had gotten married, eight years ago? I was already a mess, and I hadn't even gotten out of bed.

I looked out the window; it was raining.

Perfect.

Fixing breakfast seemed tedious; taking the boys to school felt exhausting. When I drove away from their school, my phone rang. It was my sister-in-law. She asked if I was doing okay and if I wanted to meet her at the park to go for a walk or run.

I said, "Do you mind if it's raining?"

"No, do you?"

I told her no and that I'd meet her there in fifteen minutes.

I got to the park and looked around, but Jen wasn't there yet. I sat in my car in the rain, and the instant I stopped moving, the emotions crept in and tears came. I looked over at my "to do" list sitting under my purse.

Sabrina had asked me months ago to write Mark a goodbye letter. I thought that as long as I was already this down, why shouldn't

I do it now? I pulled the top sheet of the "to do" list off of the pad of paper, got my pen, and started writing.

The words flowed with ease.

My tears dropped down as the rain fell and the words flooded on the page with a vengeance. I said what I was grateful for, I told him how I felt about him when I was with him and now that he was gone, and I said we'd be okay without him.

When I got to the end of the second page, I knew the word had to be written. I ended with only one word: "Goodbye."

I looked up as Jen's car pulled up next to mine. I wiped my eyes, set the letter down on the seat, and got out of the car.

She knew what this day would be like for me. It wasn't a holiday for other people; it wasn't anything special for anyone. It was only a reminder of my loss. She walked over and held me.

"I'm so sorry, Jen."

I couldn't say anything. We ran hard. The rain splashed in our faces and washed away my tears.

~

A few days later I was lying in bed listening to the rain and writing in my diary when the phone rang. I looked at the number and was pleasantly surprised to see it was David.

"Hey there!"

I could tell he was smiling. In an aching kind of way I was, too. Maybe there were a few feelings that would take a while to dissipate. While I knew we wouldn't be together, there was still a lingering tug at my heart strings.

"Hi, Jen; are you busy?"

"No, what's up?"

"Well, I had an interesting thing happen the other day and

wanted to tell someone about it. I knew you were the only one who would get it and maybe the only one I could tell."

He seemed a little hesitant to go on, which made me wonder what in the world he was going to say.

"Okay, the other night I was imagining what it would be like to be kissing you in your house," he said.

Whoa! My heart skipped a beat, but I just said, "Uh-huh?"

"Well, right then my glasses, which had been sitting on my nightstand for hours, fell to the ground."

"Oh really?"

"Yes, and nothing had touched them."

I wondered if he wanted me to say something, but I just waited.

He said, "I think it was Mark."

I wanted to say, "Yep, I'm sure it was. He is telling you that you should get up and go do that."

But then he said, "I wondered if he was upset that I was thinking about you."

I knew he wanted some relief. He wasn't used to Mark being around like I was. It was a new experience. I gave it to him.

"I never told you, but Mark told me he was okay with me getting to know you. Maybe he just wanted you to know he was around or wanted you to tell me what you were thinking."

I could hear the relaxation come into David's voice. "Yeah, I think you are right, it was a strange experience. I didn't feel scared or anything, just curious."

"I haven't ever felt scared when he was around, either," I said.

"Thanks for telling me. I think it's cool he's hanging out with you some. I haven't heard much from him in a while."

When we said goodbye and hung up, I closed my eyes and listened to the rain. The sound of it felt comforting.

TIME BOMBS

Life without Mark in our space every day became normal. The gaping hole became intermittent potholes. The boys and I sang, danced, played, laughed, ran, yelled, hugged, and helped each other.

We became a team. They would set the table, feed the dog, get dressed, help me with projects, and hold my hand or hug me when I needed comfort. I would make them pancakes, laugh at their young jokes, tickle them, hug them fiercely and gently, and nurture them when they were hurt.

My only lingering concern was the lack of tears from either one of them. They cried on a normal basis, but not about Mark. Brannon cried when he got hurt, and Connor wept when he was frustrated and when his best friend moved to Montana. But neither of them had cried over the loss of Mark since the first week.

There was a little piece of me that was waiting for the moment when there would be a release—when the fissure would break through the ice and start a shift to a new shape. I hoped it would start sooner rather than later. I knew at some point they would have to move through their emotions. I was concerned that the later it happened, the harder, longer, and more painful the shift would be.

And then suddenly there was a crack.

One morning as we were leaving for school, Connor asked me if he could bring his camera with him in the car.

I said, "Okay."

While we were stopped at a light, I looked back and noticed Connor was playing with the buttons on his camera. When the light turned green, I took my foot off the brake and the car started to move. At the same time I heard Connor start to sob. I was confused. What was going on? I said, "Honey, what's wrong?"

I looked in the rear view mirror and saw that he had huge tears streaming down his cheeks and dripping off his chin. I was concerned he'd hurt himself, and I said with a little more urgency, "Sweetie, what is it?"

He urgently moaned through his tears. "Mommy! I think I erased *all* of the pictures of *Daddy* off my camera!"

Oh God, now? When I can't even hold him?

I slowed down but realized I was in the middle of traffic and the road was wet from the rain the night before. I couldn't stop. I felt so helpless.

I reached back between the seats and put my hand on his knee; it was all I could reach of him. He looked up at me through his tear-streaked eyes. I couldn't even hold his gaze; I had to watch the road. I didn't dare say a word for fear of interrupting his feelings and stopping the natural release.

He cried until we pulled into the school. My heart was screaming at me; I sat with the pain throbbing through the air in the car. When I slowed down, Connor was starting to breathe more normally and his tears were slowing.

We stopped, I turned the car off, and I went around to his side. I opened the door and unbuckled his seatbelt. He reached for me the way he did when he was two. I took him in my arms and held him.

After a minute he wiped his arm across his face and looked

up at me. His huge blue eyes were stained with red streaks, but he wasn't crying.

"Sweetie, we have more pictures of Daddy than you could look at in a whole day."

He furrowed his brow and said, "Really?"

"Yes, don't worry. I have lots and lots of pictures and video of Daddy."

He closed his eyes and rested his head on my shoulder. I heard a whisper: "Okay."

Less than a week later we were all three sitting on the floor in the living room watching *Kung Fu Panda*. It was the boys' favorite movie. We'd watched it several times in the past few weeks.

In one scene, a main character decided it was his time to die, and his spirit floated off with peach blossoms. Brannon looked over at me and said, "Is he going to heaven?"

It hadn't dawned on me that they might have questions about the scene. "Yes," I said.

Brannon stood up and moved onto the couch next to us. I watched him as his lower lip started to quiver. I didn't know if I should do or say anything, so I kept still and waited.

I watched in shock as he started to hit his own face up around his eyes. I got up as quickly as I could to kneel next to him. "Brannon, are you okay?"

His face was all scrunched up, and he kept hitting it. I realized he was trying to keep himself from crying.

My gut feeling was that he needed to cry to let it out, but I couldn't let him hurt himself. I had to stop him from hitting himself. I reached toward him, and as I did he moved away from me. I moved over closer to him and put my hands on his to stop him.

Then he yanked his hands out of mine. I thought he was going to stop, but then he looked down and started scratching one of his wrists really hard. Silent tears started to spill from my eyes.

I couldn't stand to watch him hurt himself. My heart squeezed in my chest. It seemed that he was trying not to feel the raw spot of emotion and was attempting to transfer the pain to his physical body.

I blurted out, "Sweetie, it's okay to cry."

He stopped moving completely. The hesitation scared me, but at least he wasn't hurting himself anymore. I took advantage of the shift and pulled him toward me, but again he pulled away.

With a deep anger in his voice he said, "You were talking about heaven!"

All I saw was hurt, frustration, and sadness. I said, "Yes, did that make you sad?"

With an even stronger fury he yelled, "Yes!"

I looked in his scared, four-year-old eyes and said, "It really is okay to be sad."

There was another hesitation, and then I witnessed a moment of softness that peeked through the anger. He moved just a fraction of an inch toward me. I took the opportunity to bring him the rest of the way into my chest and wrapped my arms around him. The tears were spilling out of both of us then. We stayed that way for several minutes until there were not any more tears. My eyes dried . . . and then his did.

THE LAST FIRST

As the one-year anniversary of Mark's death drew near, my emotions were scattered and raw. Everything seemed exaggerated; everything seemed overly meaningful; everything was set on high volume.

It was as if there was a huge clock in the back of my head screaming "TICK! TOCK!" at me each moment, waiting for something to happen . . . but I didn't quite know what.

I feared the day would be horrible, and I know my concern bled into most everything I did for several weeks.

Two days before the anniversary, the boys talked me into going to a new hamburger place by our house. As we drove out of the drive-thru they convinced me to park in the parking lot while they watched their movie in the car.

As they were eating I leaned back in the front seat to relax for a moment. I finished my hamburger and was eating some french fries when I heard Connor say, "Mommy, why did you turn off the video?"

I thought maybe he had hit the remote or something, because I hadn't touched anything. Then I realized the lights on the dash had gone out and finally, that the car battery was dead.

I silently lay my head on the steering wheel. I felt like a rag doll, like I couldn't move. I thought, "The boys shouldn't have to see me this frail." But I couldn't help it.

I picked up the phone and dialed Jeremy's number to see if he could come jump-start the car. He said normally he would, but that he and Jen were going out to dinner and were waiting for the sitter to get there in a few minutes. He suggested I call the roadside assistance we had through our insurance.

Then to my amazement he said, "I did go jump start Dad's car this morning, though. You two!"

My dad's car battery went dead too in the same day? How strange.

I had always believed our emotions and energy might have an effect on our physical surroundings. Was that what was going on? That morning a year ago had been so hard on my dad, too. Maybe . . .

The boys both told me they were still hungry, so we went back in and I got them each another burger while we waited for help to arrive. As soon as we got back in the car, the roadside assistance arrived. We were driving down the road in less than fifteen minutes. Okay . . . I made it so far . . .

⌒

The night before the one-year anniversary I didn't want to go to bed. I sat in my office and worked for several hours. Finally, I knew I couldn't stay up much longer, so I went into my bedroom.

When I walked in I noticed a piece of paper on my bed. I hadn't seen it before. I walked over and picked it up. I turned it over and read, "Hey, Jen, I just wanted to let you know I am thinking about you. I realize tomorrow is a big day, but tomorrow is a *good* day. A year ago was crap; not tomorrow. Take some time to enjoy your boys and realize how far you've come in a year. You're a strong woman, but if you need anything, just ask. I love you. Jeremy." ·

There aren't words to describe what that letter meant to me.

~

I tossed and turned for hours. When I finally slept, it was fitful at best. I awoke several times during the night and then again at six in the morning I decided to get out of bed and take a shower.

I got dressed and went into Connor's room, not unlike a year ago. This time he was not awake, and it was raining and very dark outside. I decided to sit in his room. I waited for about five minutes in the darkness and silence, listening to the rain hit the window. I heard Connor stir, so I stood up and went to the side of his bed.

He looked up at me and said, "Hi, Mommy."

I sat down on his bed and laid my head on his body. "Good morning, sweetie."

He got up and we walked downstairs, hand in hand.

While Brannon slept, Connor fed the dog, and I got breakfast going. Then I heard Brannon coming downstairs. I couldn't wait until he got there; I started toward the stairs. As he got to the bottom he walked toward me, and my heart caught in my throat.

He was still here.

Thank you, Mark.

I walked over to him and kneeled down. I put my arms around him and said, "Morning, sweetie. I love you."

"I love you too, Mommy."

I looked up at the clock. It was 7:48. My body relaxed. We'd made it.

~

That night Jen and Jeremy came over with Dad for dinner. We had pizza and then sat around the kitchen table talking.

It had been pouring most of the day, but during dinner the clouds were starting to break apart. As everyone got up to go home we heard Connor excitedly exclaim, "Look!"

We all walked to the front of the house and looked out at a double rainbow that was right in front of our home. I stood there in awe.

〜

The next morning I was working in my office and the phone rang. I was in the middle of something, so I grabbed it and quickly said, "Hello."

It was quiet for a second, then I heard Mark's sister Karen say, "Hey Jen."

She sounded hesitant to say anything.

After a minute I said, "It's ok, what is it?"

She said, "He's here a lot."

I smiled.

"He even helps me get to work on time. He tells me which way to drive to miss traffic and hit the green lights."

We both laughed.

〜

The next day Mark's dad and sisters all arrived at our house. We were going to go to Sam's ranch where Mark had hunted with his best friends for over twenty-five years. Sam and I had planned a small gathering of Mark's closest friends and family to celebrate him after one year.

The weather was perfectly sunny: not a cloud in the sky and

about sixty degrees. It was the only day in a fourteen-day window of time that it didn't rain.

About thirty of Mark's closest friends and family members met, sat, hugged, smiled, laughed, and cried together for about five hours. Before we started the "formal" gathering, I told Connor and Brannon that some adults were going to talk about Daddy and that they could listen or go play with the other kids. Brannon played with the other kids. Connor followed me to the tables. However, I watched in confusion as he headed straight for David's lap.

It unnerved me a little that Connor chose someone else to sit with during this emotional time. I watched him closely as people spoke about Mark; he seemed to be okay. I saw David say something in Connor's ear. Connor nodded his head. I wondered what David had said.

I felt mixed emotions watching them. I was happy that Connor felt close to a man who wasn't family, especially one who had cared so much about Mark. I knew David loved having Connor there with him. He probably felt extremely honored that he chose him to sit with.

I was also happy that David and I had remained friends. But my heart ached watching them. I'd had a few dates with other men and knew I'd eventually find someone to share my life with, but I still had a soft spot in my heart for David. He'd had a special place in my life during the last year. Watching him interact so closely with my child was a sharp reminder of the feelings I'd had.

After several people had told funny stories about Mark, Randy's wife, Amy, started to speak.

She looked directly at Connor and said, "Connor, I knew your daddy before he married your mommy. I wanted you to know that he was so excited to marry your mommy. And after they got married we helped them move into their new home. It was a special place because they knew they wanted to have kids there. And they did; they had you.

"I also wanted to tell you that your daddy talked about you all the time. He loved telling stories about every little new thing you did when you were growing up. He loved you so much. He was so proud of you."

I watched Connor while Amy was talking. He had sat up and was paying very close attention to her. His eyes were wide, and he had a grin on his face like I hadn't seen in a while. I knew then that the entire event was for that moment.

After everyone finished sharing we began to disperse. I walked over to the urn that had Mark's ashes in it. We were planning on spreading them at the ranch since it had been his favorite place.

I had a fleeting thought that I should check to make sure the ashes were in the box. I'd never opened it, so I wasn't absolutely sure. The thought seemed silly, but it nagged at me nonetheless.

Eventually the idea got the better of me, and I reached down to lift the lid. As I pulled on it, nothing happened; there wasn't any movement at all. It was like the lid was glued down. Then with a shock, I realized it was.

A flood of emotions and thoughts and sensations slammed into my body and mind. I wondered if I was pulling on it wrong. But no, I wasn't.

Thoughts tumbled through my mind: "What are we going to do now?" "Are you kidding?"

"I'm going to have to call the funeral home and see what I can do to open it . . ." "What is really going on?"

As I stood there with the last thought, I took a few breaths to calm down a little.

I heard, "I want to stay with you and the boys."

The boys and I sat at my desk looking through pictures of Mark. Each of them was picking out the ones they wanted to put in their new photo albums. I was telling them the stories about each picture and writing down notes to add to the album.

I looked at Mark's eyes in one of the photographs. They were the same loving, gentle eyes I'd always known, but it seemed that now there was a depth to them I could see even better.

I saw so many gifts of kindness and love shining out through his eyes, as clearly as if he were standing in the room. I'd taken that picture, and he'd been looking straight at me when I did. However, I appreciated and loved him more now than I ever had.

I looked over at the two most precious gifts he'd ever given me and saw our future in their eyes.

Dear Connor and Brannon,

Be everything you want to be.

Laugh, love, live, smile, play, give.

Be kind and be there for each other.

I love you more than life itself.

Mark Hawkins, Dad

ACKNOWLEDGMENTS

There have been hundreds of people, family, friends, even strangers who have lifted me and the boys up since February 2009.

That said, there are a few who yanked me out of the depths of the black hole, some unknowingly. Without you, my life would not be what it is.

Thank you, in the order of your incredible presence after that moment, Deb Ingram, Nathalie D'Alessandro, Roger Brannon, Lydia Rudy, Connor and Brannon Hawkins, Abby Brannon, Cheryl Franck, Connie Randmaa, Jeremy Brannon, Ray Hawkins, Kathy Throop, Sam Schaefer, Juri Randmaa, Jennifer Brannon, LeeAnne Randmaa, Alissa Chasen, Tabitha Rozeboom, Jayne Johnson, Sabrina Kindell, Joe Diosana, David Haynes, Wells Mason, Amy Hairr, Rick Perkal, and Jerry Stocking.

Your spirits shine very brightly in my life, and because of that, also have a profound effect on the lives of Connor and Brannon. Thank you. Thank you.

Photo by Amy Melsa

ABOUT THE AUTHOR

Jennifer Hawkins grew up in Southern California. For more than a decade, she was a competitive swimmer, earning a spot at the Olympic trials in 1988. In 1991, she moved to Texas, where she became a successful realtor, investor, and author. In 2000, she met her husband Mark and soon after started a family.

Jennifer still lives in Texas with her two boys and the many friends that add richness to her life every day.